S

Swimming for the Disabled

Association of Swimming Therapy

Adam & Charles Black
London

ISBN 0-7136-2624-0

Published by
A & C Black (Publishers) Limited,
35 Bedford Row, London WC1R 4JH

Text set in 10 on 12 pt VIP Times, printed by photolithography and bound in Great Britain at The Pitman Press, Bath.

First published 1981
Reprinted 1984

Acknowledgements
Our thanks are due to many who are too numerous to mention by name. However, we do wish to record our thanks to David Cooper, Candy McMahon for her typing, Jim Kibart for the diagrams in the physics chapter, and Stephen Harper and Bill Latto of Town and Country Productions for their painstaking photographic work. Above all we are deeply indebted to Haro for generously giving his excellent drawings.

The A.S.T. wishes gratefully to acknowledge the enormous contribution made by James McMillan M.B.E. to *Swimming for the Disabled*.

The A.S.T. and the publishers have made every effort to satisfy the legal requirements of copyright in material used in this book; nonetheless persons who may have a further copyright claim should apply to the publishers.

Contents

List of Photographs

Preface

I am delighted to have the opportunity of writing the preface to this publication. The Sports Council is fully aware of the enormous value of swimming, particularly to people with disabilities, and has supported its promotion in a variety of ways for many years.

The main reason that people swim is to enjoy it. It is fun, it is good exercise and it engenders a feeling of well-being. For many people it is much more: it allows freedom of movement which is denied on dry land; it provides an element of risk and challenge often lacking in an otherwise sheltered life. Swimming encompasses so many activities; long distance, recreation, competition, synchronised to music, games and, most important, a social programme as a member of the club.

The Association of Swimming Therapy has long been in the forefront of developing swimming for disabled people. The Halliwick method is practised worldwide and the film *Water Free* has won many awards, but the most important work is on the poolside in the many clubs where more and more people with all types of disability are taught and encouraged to swim by a vast number of able-bodied enthusiasts.

It is particularly appropriate that *Swimming for the Disabled* should appear in 1981, the International Year of Disabled People, when the Sports Council, together with all the sporting, disability, voluntary and statutory organisations, are running a 'Sport for All – Disabled People' campaign. This book will make an important contribution to the campaign and will inform many people of how they can help. I wish it well.

Dick Jeeps, C.B.E. *Chairman, The Sports Council*

Chapter One
Introduction

This book is about having fun in the water. It is mainly concerned with disabled people but it will help those of all ages who are learning to swim or to relish the joy of independence in the water in safety.

Swimming for the Disabled describes a method of teaching water ability to the disabled which can ultimately be traced back to the principles of Archimedes, the laws of Newton and the equation of Bernoulli. It is based on the scientific fact that a body floats in water. In practice the method owes its foundation to James McMillan, M.B.E., President Emeritus of the Association of Swimming Therapy (A.S.T.). (The structure of the A.S.T. is described on p.140.) The 'Halliwick method' derived its name from the Halliwick School for Girls, Southgate, London, where in 1949 Mr McMillan developed the method by adapting scientific and hydrodynamic principles to the behaviour of the human body in water. The Halliwick method is now practised in over 85 clubs in Great Britain and in many countries throughout the world. It is not a rigid concept but is always being refined and evolving in the light of experience and practice.

We are principally concerned with disabled people, who suffer some physical or mental handicap whether from birth or acquired; but we should all remember that no-one is perfect – some excellent golfers have a 'handicap'– and so this borderline is often difficult to define precisely. The miracle of water is that it blurs this separation, or distinction, frequently into invisibility. For we are all more equal in water; crutches and wheelchairs are laid aside and we float at roughly the same level and so enjoy equality of level and 'level speaking'.

In water disabilities are less visible. Water is critical of two factors only: *shape* and *density*. It is very supportive and when used correctly it can stimulate or relax the disabled swimmer.

This book will, we hope, encourage those whose lives are restricted by their handicap to take to the water and broaden the horizons of their existence. A handicap shortens horizons – for some these extend no further than the walls of a room or wheelchair: it can be like a prison with entire dependence on others for movement. But in water it is all different and with a little courage and determination total independence in the water can be acquired. The sense of freedom and achievement will act as a great moral and spiritual boost to everyday life.

Some of the disabled become good instructors. For convenience we term those that are disabled 'swimmers' and the rest 'helpers'. And here should be stressed the fun and sense of achievement enjoyed by the helpers in helping their swimmers. The joy of swimmer and helper is equal: and the huge inspiration of the swimmers' perseverance, often in the face of the greatest handicaps, encourages others in their own lives to greater things.

We hope that this book will be read widely – well beyond those members who attend their weekly club session at the local swimming pool. The medical and para-medical professions will read much here that they know already, but will also find many ideas that will be stimulating and may provoke a desire to join in. It is just this cross-fertilisation of knowledge and practice from those with a wide range of backgrounds that has in the past yielded maximum progress, and will do so in the future. To list other potential readers would involved a rollcall of thanks to those who enable the movement to go forward: baths staff, Swimming Teachers Association, Voluntary Lifeguards, St John's Ambulance Brigade, 'first aiders', public officials, Rotary and all those club helpers who make for a successful and happy club – to name but a few. Some fear that this publication will result in armchair experts who know the book by heart but never enter the water; to avoid this, we must stress that practice and water experience is of paramount importance. This cannot be exaggerated.

The word 'fun' has been emphasised. For young people this is likely to mean games, races, gala competitions, open water swims and diving. Others will not be so ambitious, and the sheer exhilaration of discarding the impedimenta necessary on land and entering the supporting water with the goal of independence will be enough. Progress, through the badge tests etc., should be encouraged, but in some cases, for one reason or another, it may be impossible.

Although much of this will have substantial remedial effects, that is not our aim. This is about recreation.

There are areas of this work, which we can only touch upon briefly, where we can expect considerable future development. In no field is this more true than the Gemini Scheme. This involves the teaching of the method to senior school pupils during their latter terms with a view to broadening their education and encouraging them to carry on a sociable activity after leaving school by helping the disabled (under supervision). This will enable them to instruct the disabled schoolchild in their own area.

In Britain today, happily, there are many organisations concerned with swimming for the disabled. For some this multiplicity may be considered confusing and even wasteful. The efforts of the various organisations are monitored by the Sports Council of the National Co-ordinating Committee of Swimming for the Disabled.

The Amateur Swimming Association (A.S.A.), Association of Swimming Therapy (A.S.T.), the National Association of Swimming Clubs for the Handicapped (N.A.S.C.H.), Swimming Teachers Association and Royal Life Society and other bodies are currently working together on the Co-ordinating Committee. In their efforts the interests of disabled people themselves must always be paramount, for without the example and inspiration of their courage and cheerfulness little would be achieved.

Chapter Two
Safety and Handling

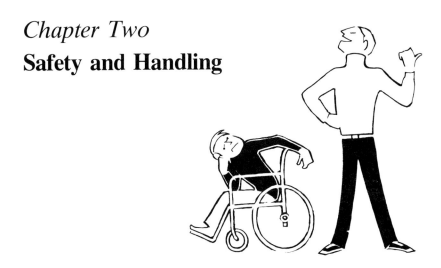

GENERAL

The safety and handling of a swimmer is fundamental; for if a swimmer is hurt at your club much is lost, and if he is unhappy about the way he is handled he may never come again. Here is something of a battle of hearts and minds; it is not sufficient that disabled people are safe; they must *feel* safe, both when handled on the side and in the water. Helpers should aim to earn confidence, minimise fuss, and never make disabled people feel they are being a nuisance. Laughter and fun are great assets here.

Helpers should selflessly adjust their minds to think how disabled people feel – and perhaps remember what it was like when you had a broken leg plastered up from top to bottom. Disabled people are equally entitled to take risks; but it must be of their own free will and not as the result of someone else's negligence or misunderstanding.

BEFORE AND AFTER ENTERING THE POOL

You may start as an escort collecting the swimmer from home, providing transport to the pool and then helping your swimmer to undress in the changing rooms. Remember that the aim is independence and that the object is to give the minimum of help, thus

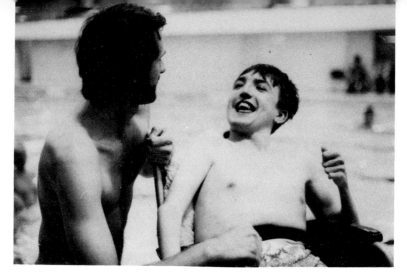

1. 'Level speaking' with a wheelchair swimmer.

encouraging self-confidence, a sense of achievement and progress. The frequent temptation is to do everything for a disabled person because it is quicker and the bus is waiting – avoid this. Remember that the aids for his disability give assistance that the swimmer is used to, so do not interfere too much, though you should ensure that the swimmer does not slip and that the way is clear for a wheelchair. The most dangerous place is the hard, wet, slippery surface of the poolside, particularly after leaving the pool. Pay particular care in this area. Above all, think how best you can be helpful and appreciate that the more experience you have the more valuable your help will be. Don't be shy – talk to and discuss how to undress the swimmer – he will have the best ideas of how he can be helped.

The blind will need to have the layout of the pool explained; they may be much confused if there are alterations; the mentally handicapped may be unaware of danger and require intelligent supervision. A particular point should be made concerning sensitive skin, especially in those with little or no feeling – ensure that feet are placed on wheelchair footrests and do not trail or hit doors; damage thus sustained will take a long while to heal.

Lifting
Helpers are in as much danger here as swimmers. Don't try to be a Hercules but seek help – it is safer for all with two or more helpers and

the swimmer will be more confident. Lifters must bend their knees and use their strong leg muscles with a straight back in a synchronised lift (see photograph 2). Avoid jerks and keep close together with the firm wrist-to-wrist grip. The 'transit seat' is ideal as this enables as many as four lifters to work to the comfort of the swimmer. Wear suitable shoes that will not slip. The best hold (see photograph 3) involves keeping the swimmer's limbs together, with both lifters' arms overlapping at the back and hands overlapped beneath the legs (a wrist hold) – don't hold fingers or hands – and, above all, keep your back straight to avoid Britain's commonest ache!

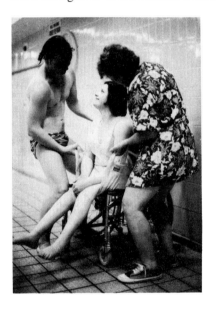

2. *(Left)* Helpers – bend your knees and spare your backs!
3. *(Above)* Safe and secure overhand grip for lifters.

Changing clothes

An open communal changing room without cubicles has been found ideal, for better club spirit is fostered and those who need help can readily be seen. By now you will have some idea of the wide range of helpers needed in a successful club, and in this area and others the services of the Red Cross, St John's Ambulance, Boy Scouts, Girl Guides and Task Force may well augment your numbers.

Getting changed can be made easier by the swimmer coming in

sensible clothing – a minimum of complicated fastenings, shoes without laces and Velcro in place of buttons can speed things up considerably. Clothes should always be piled neatly to avoid loss. A good general principle is once more to listen to the swimmers and encourage them increasingly to dress and undress themselves – and even help each other. For children, a bench or table covered with a towel to avoid slipping and for warmth is best, and parents will often help here. Generally, start at the feet and work upwards, ascertain balance ability through head control, and remember that rotation (which is so important in the water) is an aid to dressing and undressing. Put the handicapped limb in first and don't be shy about drying private parts – wet underclothes are a sad way to end a happy swim.

It is wise to ensure that there is always a helper in both male and female changing rooms when swimmers are present.

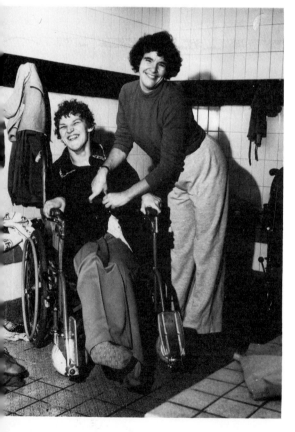

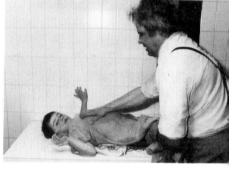

4. *(Left)* Encourage the disabled to help each other – it can be fun too.

5. *(Above)* Dressing and undressing can often be best carried out on a table.

Moving

Many of the handicapped are quite capable of moving unaided but will require help with the unusual obstacles of the pool, such as doors and showers. Some can, through their ingenuity and determination, manoeuvre themselves from a wheelchair down onto the footrest and thus to the poolside unaided. Helpers should watch out for those who are being over-ambitious or foolhardy. Two helpers should lift the swimmer from his wheelchair. They should face each other, move away the footrests, ensure the brake is applied and support the swimmer under his arm, holding his hand in the helper's palm – the helper thus has a second arm free for further assistance if needed. Where possible, encourage the swimmer to stand momentarily on his feet. The same hold can be applied to someone sitting on the poolside; in this instance the feet should be blocked and the swimmer encouraged to push upward with his leg muscles to stand up.

There will inevitably be time spent waiting at the poolside, so towels should be available for warmth and adequate seating provided. Towels can prevent slipping on the poolside and protect sensitive skins.

ENTERING THE POOL

The helper is in the pool in a well-balanced position, feet apart, knees bent and one foot in front of the other, reaching up with his palms supporting the swimmer around his shoulder blades (see photograph 6). The swimmer should be sitting on the edge of the pool with his palms resting on the helper's shoulders. Helpers! This can be a tense moment and all your encouragement ('How warm the water is') may be needed. Don't splash, and keep your elbows in so as to envelop those who feel most insecure. For children, choose a quiet corner of the pool and maintain eye-to-eye contact with your swimmer to block his view of a vast expanse of water and to ensure he keeps his head well forward. This is the first stage. Some will need poolside support from the back. If the swimmer is a stiff adult, ensure that he enters the pool in water deep enough to prevent jarring his feet on the bottom.

The helper should select a depth of water where he can stand steadily, remembering that a depth of water is a 'cushion' for the swimmer as he enters. As soon as the swimmer is in the pool, start an

6. Entry to the water – the first stage, with maximum support behind the shoulder blades.
7. Entry to the water – the next stage towards disengagement. Watch your swimmer.

8. Entry to the water – as confidence grows disengagement is almost complete.

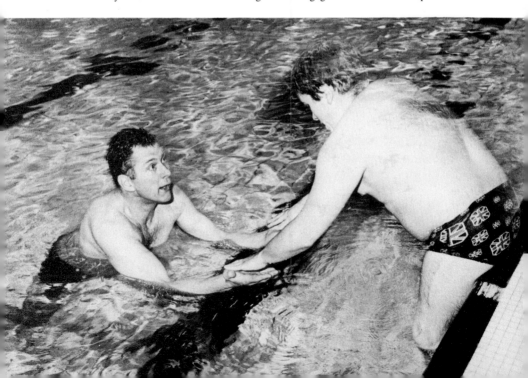

activity and talk – encourage blowing bubbles and ask a few questions – in this way any fear is quickly forgotten. Other methods of entry from palms (helper's upwards) to palms (see photograph 7) can then progress towards the goal of total disengagement – we discourage use of the steps as there are more hard surfaces around to cause injury.

Perhaps the greatest danger is that the swimmer will throw his head back and hit it on the side; so exhort your swimmer to 'look at me' and thus keep his head forward.

9. Entry to the water – a different method involving a combined rotation.
10. Entry to the water – rotations. After aiding entry with one arm the helper moves away from the side of the swimmer.
11. Entry to the water – with total disengagement and horizontal rotation.

Handling: how not to do it! spot the errors

HOLDS IN THE WATER

As a general rule, aim towards minimum support and remember that the water itself is supportive. So, the more the swimmer is in the water the greater the upthrust to support him and the more stable he will be. Don't grip, and discourage being gripped (especially intertwining fingers) – tension increases density and hinders flotation. Always leave the swimmer's head free as no other part of the body so readily facilitates balance.

Initially the helper's hold should be firm, not rough; this will instil confidence. Later it can be relaxed and support reduced. Swimmers and helpers should constantly ensure that all hands are always under the water.

Most importantly, keep a close watch on your swimmer at all times.

Kangaroo jumps:
you may not do as well as this but try

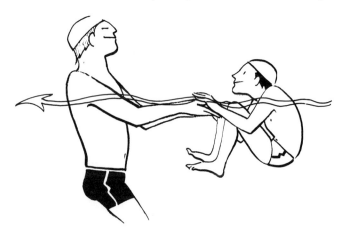

Vertical holds

Face to face Having entered the water looking at the helper, the 'face-to-face' position naturally comes first. The helper's upturned flat palms support the swimmer's downturned flat palms. This hold is used in Kangaroo Jumps (see foot of previous page) as the helper walks backwards across the pool.

Bicycle hold Helper faces swimmer's back with arms forward between swimmer's elbows and body, palms as in face to face hold. This is an excellent hold for securing a swimmer who needs much support: the helper's palms can be raised if the swimmer falls forward and the helper's chest can be pressed forward to restore the swimmer's balance if he falls back.

As a progression the helper reduces support by moving his palms to the swimmer's waist. This is the hold used in the game known as Poached Eggs (see p. 102).

12. 'With a little help from my friend' – the bicycle support position.

Chair position There is very little holding in the chair position. The helper balances in the water, knees bent and feet apart, and gently encourages the swimmer to sit, bob and balance on his knee. Helpers should imagine they are bouncing a large ball on their knee. The swimmer should have his hands forward 'on the table' and use his head to maintain balance. If steadying of the swimmer is needed, the helper will put his palms on the swimmer's waist. This position is used for Musical Chairs (see p. 115).

The horizontal position flows from here; by the call 'go to bed/look at the ceiling', whereupon the swimmer puts his head back, the helper steps backwards and takes up the horizontal hold.

The back float position: the helper may give extra support with palms in the small of the back of the swimmer; the chair position is achieved from here by the swimmer putting his head forward so that his feet drop

The back float position: frequent error of new helpers! Allow your swimmer to float naturally with minimum support

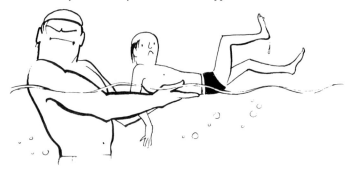

The (wrong) back float position: incorrect handling means the swimmer is unable to appreciate the support of the water

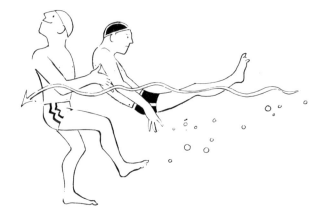

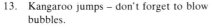

13. Kangaroo jumps – don't forget to blow bubbles.

14. Instilling confidence and giving maximum support to the new swimmer.

Horizontal hold

Support from the helper should be with his palms in the small of the swimmer's back. The helper's head must be level with the swimmer's head, and this will facilitate a good flow of words of encouragement and exhortation to the swimmer – the swimmer may also rest his head on the helper's shoulder.

The helper thus walks backwards across the pool; initially the swimmer is a 'canoe', progressing to kicking with his legs as a 'motor boat' and then to 'wriggling round the rocks' when the helper's hands are on the swimmer's waist (see p. 98).

Long arm hold (vertical or horizontal)

This may be used in line or circle formation – once again the helper's flat palms are upturned and the swimmer's downturned, on extended arms. This hold is used in Ring a Ring o' Roses (vertical), Rag Dolls (horizontal) and Shooting the Rapids (horizontal and vertical).

Short arm hold (vertical or horizontal)
This is a variant of the long arm hold for swimmers who need more
support. The helper, with palms to palms as before, tucks his elbow
between his swimmer's elbow and body. Swimmer's and helper's
inside forearms are thus together so as to form a reassuring
togetherness – like a concertina. This hold may be used in circles
(Ring a Ring o' Roses, Football Match, Ding Dong Bell) or in line
(Rag Dolls).

With increased confidence and ability, the short arm hold can
extend to a long arm hold by the helper sliding palms (always
maintaining contact) along the swimmer's arms.

15. A group in extended arm (or trying to extend
    arms!) back float position.
16. Exit from the water – the horizontal lift. Note
    (a) swimmer's crossed arms; (b) helper's palms
    downwards to grip the poolside and protect knuckles;
    (c) special arm protection of swimmer's head.

GETTING OUT

The principal aim in getting a swimmer out of the water and onto the
poolside is the safety and comfort of the swimmer. Nor should the
safety of the helper be forgotten. Use of the bath steps is to be
discouraged as a slip may result in injury sustained from the tiled
poolside or metal rails.

We use two methods:

Vertical

This method is well illustrated in photographs 17, 18, 19. The helper, whose palms are supporting the swimmer's waist, should exhort the swimmer to get his chest well up onto the poolside. The rhythm and upthrust of the water to the call of '1, 2 ... 3' will help to achieve this. From here the swimmer should energetically wriggle further till his hips are on the side before rolling over into a sitting position.

Horizontal

For those swimmers who need more assistance three helpers are required. The swimmer lies flat and still, parallel to the pool side, facing upwards with his arms crossed on his chest. The helpers should select a depth of water that minimizes strain on their backs.

The three helpers stand shoulder to shoulder, facing the poolside. Their palms should face downwards for protection and particular

17. Exit from the water – 'One, two, three ... and I'm up' – or half way at least.
18. Exit from the water – the next stage; 'A few more wriggles and I'll be there'. Note the swimmer's legs are supported on the helper's shoulder.
19. Exit from the water – 'Success! Now I can turn over into the sitting position'.

care should be taken of the swimmer's head to prevent injury. The middle helper is the leader and should be the strongest. Using the upthrust of the water, and with a smooth strong rhythm, the swimmer is lifted up and down in the water to gather momentum, to the calls of '1, 2 ... 3'. On '3' a strong co-ordinated force upwards is exerted to lift the swimmer onto the poolside, aiming the buttocks gently into the waiting 'transit seat'.

Bathside helpers should then swivel the swimmer round to a sitting position, ensuring that his feet are protected as they clear the poolside. The swimmer may now be lifted into his wheelchair.

Chapter Three
Progress of a Swimmer

To progress, a swimmer requires the courage and initiative to attend a club and enter the water; with assistance from helpers, it should then be possible to progress to independence, water safety and, later, even competitive swimming and possibly a Channel swim!

Progress is a constant feature of everyday life but in sport the striving for improvement is more intense. Happily, with the increased popularity of swimming, local authorities are now more willing to give 'pool time' as part of their social services programme for the disabled.

At a club session, one of the most important helpers should be in charge of the personal progress records of each swimmer – for without such written record development and achievement, or the lack of it, can never be properly established; memory is just not good enough. A photograph on each sheet is a great help when a new recorder takes over, and facilitates discussion at helpers' meetings.

BADGE TESTS

These are measures of progress and can be worn (sewn on the swimsuit) with pride by those who have passed. They represent to all others a known level of achievement: swimmers who have not passed their 'green', for instance, should not be allowed in the deep end unaccompanied. The tests established a level of safety and the importance of the 'green' and 'blue' should be maintained. Favouritism should be avoided by involving examiners from another affiliated club; this brings the 'badge system' into line with other national swimming awards where external examination is mandatory.

20. A group studies details of games and badge tests during a club session.

Experienced club helpers may invigilate the first two – 'red' and 'yellow' – badge tests. Each test indicates real progress so that the swimmer who passes his 'yellow' should have control of rotations, whilst entering the pool from the sitting position and in the water so as to return to the safe breathing position. Jumping unaided for ten metres ensures a fair degree of head control and sitting on the bottom will show a good mental adjustment to water. A further advance, within the same test, is picking up an object from the bottom where obviously one has to keep one's eyes open under water.

The final 'blue' test can be thought of as a build-up to the A.S.A. personal survival awards and involves swimming further and with a different stroke. The swimmer must also swim in clothes and demonstrate manoeuvrability. Helpers as well as swimmers should be able to pass their 'green' test and be capable of backward and forward somersaults.

Picking the plate off the pool bottom:
eyes open for water confidence –
part of the yellow badge test

Once a swimmer has won all his A.S.T. badges he should be encouraged to enter for the A.S.A. or other awards. Ultimately, those who achieve a high level of competence could join the Royal Life Saving Society and so put their skills to good use under the Society's guidance.

1 **Red Test** (non-swimmer)
   a Enter the water unaided from a sitting position to a helper.
   b Blow a plastic 'egg' (support from behind only if necessary) for 10 metres.
   c Perform, aided in the normal manner, kangaroo jumps for a distance of 10 metres.
   d Perform a forward recovery with a minimum of aid.

2 **Yellow Test** (non-swimmer)
   a Enter from the bathside to a stable position in the water unassisted in any way.
   b Sit on the bottom of the bath, or submerge satisfactorily, and demonstrate the ability to breathe out under water.
   c Kangaroo jump, or walk, unaided for 10 metres.
   d Demonstrate a horizontal roll in either direction with the minimum of aid.
   e Pick up a plate, or like object, from at least 1 metre of water.
   f Perform either a forward or backward somersault with the minimum of aid.

3 **Green Test** (swimmer) (to be independently examined)
   a Swim a distance of 10 metres by any method.
   b Perform unaided: i. forward recovery; ii. rolling recovery.
   c Float motionlessly for at least 10 seconds *or* mushroom float for 3 seconds.
   d Demonstrate the ability to enter the water head first and unaided.
   e Somersault in the water either forward or backward unaided.
   f Against swirling water, *either* get out over the side unaided, *or*, if physically impossible, maintain a safe position from which assistance can be given.
   g Tread water for at least 60 seconds.

4   **Blue Test** (swimmer) (to be independently examined)
  a Swim unaided, by any method, for 100 metres.
  b Scull a figure-of-eight within an area of 10 metres by 5 metres.
  c Plunge a distance of swimmer's own height plus 2 metres.
  d Demonstrate ability to swim 10 metres using alternative stroke to that used in (a).
  e Perform one of the following: i wash tube; ii rolling log, iii water wheel.

COMPETITION

Herein lies a major tool for progress, common to all walks of life. This is particularly so amongst the young who can often be exhorted or cajoled to greater achievement by pitting one against another – 'Look at Johnny; he's kangaroo jumping higher than you' – and thus stimulating natural bravado.

Friendly trickery can work wonders. Swimmer A who always beat B swore he would never go into the deep end. The helper made them both work their way by hands along the edge of the pool to the deep end. Standing in the middle of the pool he exhorted: 'Race to me'. Swimmer A won and only realised later, when told, that he'd swum in the deep end.

Next come informal width and then length races with handicaps (noted from the record sheets). At the appropriate stage swimmers may compete in club galas to which neighbouring clubs can be invited; and then there are regional and national competitions. The League table is run throughout the year between teams from individual clubs at regional or national level.

Swimming outside the relative security of the indoor pool is also encouraged. This naturally leads onto ½ and 1 mile races in supervised open water swims and in 1970 culminated in the fastest team relay across the English Channel.

PROGRESS TROPHIES

Quite apart from the badge awards and gala prizes it is a good idea to make progress awards within the club. These awards can be made, as a result of club helpers' meetings and discussions, to those who have tried hard and made progress (relative to their ability) in the year. Thus the achievement of those other than the old hands who carry off the competition prizes is acknowledged and encouraged.

GENERAL PROGRESS

Progress need not be competitive, and its results should enhance the swimmer's ordinary life. By the fact that the swimmer is taking what is usually regular exercise in the water, it must result in increased stamina and movements, deeper breathing, and relaxation. It can also help by allowing the disabled to mix with the helpers and others, and by making any disability less noticeable. There is, moreover, the sense of progress to independence and another area in which the disabled can express themselves alongside the non-disabled and thus lose that feeling of being different.

Chapter Four
Stage 1: Adjustment to Water

It is essential for everyone, disabled or not, to become adapted to the water if they are to be happy independent swimmers. All too often a person can be seen 'swimming' in a pool; they tend to use a crawl stroke with head and face kept well out of the water. The expression on their face changes from an expression of 'Look, I'm swimming' to one of anxiety as their face is submerged or splashed by the water. The water-happy swimmer should be unperturbed by splashes, intentional or otherwise.

Even before a swimmer can actually propel himself through water, it is essential that he become water-confident. Each swimmer is aided by a helper to achieve balance in the water, working first in the upright and then in the horizontal position, changing from creatures of land to swimmers in the water.

DEVELOPMENT OF CONFIDENCE

During the first eighteen months of life the developing child goes through the following stages: lying – rolling – sitting – crawling – kneeling – standing; and as balance is achieved, the child learns to walk. Some of the disabled spend considerably more time in achieving these goals, and some never do – on land.

Working in the water is the reverse. The swimmer first learns to gain his balance in the vertical position – progression is made through the sitting position into the floating position. *No aids* are used except for the hands of the helper. The helper's hands are used to help balance the swimmer's body in the water to a degree that is necessary and no more. They should never be used to push the swimmer above his natural floating position. All supports are maintained using flat hands and are ideally held at the level of the centre of gravity.

To aid the transition from land to water, everyday terms are used such as 'sitting in the chair', 'lying in bed', and 'bicycle rides'. Through games and activities the swimmer is encouraged to relax so that his mind may be diverted from the alien substance, water.

Activities are initially in the upright position. These include walking with the helper in front of the swimmer, the helper walking backwards; kangaroo jumps, where the same position is adopted but the swimmer jumps, blowing bubbles as his face nears the water; 'bicycling' with the helper supporting the swimmer from behind, or blowing and turning over a 'poached egg' across the pool. By gradually sitting the swimmer 'in the chair' (see p. 21), and persuading him to put his head back, a horizontal position can be attained. In the early stages, the progression to the horizontal position must not be rushed. Remember that many of the disabled have spent a long time becoming upright and may become discouraged if they are made to feel that they are losing what they have fought hard to learn.

Activities used to help swimmers gain confidence on their backs include 'canoes', 'motor boats' and 'wriggling' (see p. 98). Here the support is by the horizontal hold using flat hands at the hips/waist level which is the balance point of most bodies.

With both the vertical and horizontal activities the swimmer is introduced to the effects of turbulence and upthrust, in many cases without being aware of them. While these effects are quietly becoming second nature to the swimmer, he is introduced to rolling, lateral, combined and further vertical rotations. Progression to independent swimming is often very slow but can frequently be

Artificial aids can unbalance a swimmer, upset his confidence in the water's support and ... if they leak ...

achieved. Once this has taken place the swimmer has the freedom of
the pool (medical conditions allowing) and so has the opportunity to
make independent decisions.

Using various activities, the swimmer can be made to feel at home
in the water, without even a hint at actually swimming. All the time
new activities are being introduced, the helper is allowing the
swimmer to make progress. Each new activity is described or
demonstrated to him. At first the helper gives the swimmer a great

21.   The water-happy swimmer in the back float and safe breathing position.

deal of support. After repetition the swimmer may find that the exercise is easier to control. A good helper at this stage can feel this through his fingers and support can be reduced slightly so as to make the swimmer more independent and the activity more difficult. This can progress until eventually the swimmer has no physical contact during the exercise. We call this 'disengagement'.

Disengagement is exemplified in kangaroo jumps. Initially full support should be given to a small child who clings to the helper, gradually progressing on two hands, one hand, and, finally no support at all. When a swimmer is totally disengaged, it can be seen that the swimmer is responsible for his own balance, be it in the vertical or horizontal plane. In fact for many of the disabled it requires more skill to walk in the water than it takes to swim, especially if they are unable to walk on land.

Disengagement takes place when the helper recognises that the swimmer has mastered the skill concerned. It is important that all helpers can recognise when this moment has arrived. Helpers will know this from hard experience and their own adjustment to water.

With careful handling and disengagement the helper can instil in the swimmer the realisation that it is the water that is doing the supporting and not the helper. If this has been put over correctly and the handling is good, all swimmers should be happy with any helper. The situation should never arise where one swimmer adamantly refuses to get into the water unless taken by a specific helper. The swimmer is then relying for confidence on the helper (who may not always be there) and not on his own ability in the water. Working in groups can help prevent this problem from starting, as swimmers move round from helper to helper in a number of activities.

Chapter Five
Stage 2: Rotations

A relaxed swimmer's body floating in water that is slightly turbulent will tend to take up a very stable position. The only problem here is that the swimmer's face may be under the water. To achieve a safe breathing position, the swimmer has to turn or rotate. From the chapter on physics we will discover that for forces in line no rotation occurs, and so to produce a rotation the swimmer must move his centre of gravity (that is, change his weight distribution) or his centre of buoyancy (change his shape under the water). As a change, or asymmetry, in the shape of the submerged body will create a roll, it is obvious that a swimmer with a physical disability that alters a 'normal' balanced shape will have an inborn tendency to roll.

In practice, there are three forms of rotation that are useful; vertical, lateral and, using part of both of these, the combined rotation. Although they are described in this order, their teaching usually follows the pattern of vertical, combined, lateral and more advanced rotations (i.e. somersaults). This is because the combined rotation introduces the lateral roll and also provides a safety measure in that the swimmer learns a method of attaining a safe breathing position should he fall in the water.

When asked to perform rotations in the water, most people will carry them out at such a rate that they are unable to describe how they were performed. It must be stressed that in teaching these rotations, they should, after initiation by the swimmer, be carried out at the speed that the water will allow, and if necessary completed by the helper. The roll consists of about ¼ initiation and maintaining shape, ½ passive roll, ¼ recovery. It is the water that does the turning; the swimmer merely changes shape and waits for the roll to occur.

VERTICAL ROTATION

This term is used to describe a head-over-heels type of rotation (also called forward rotation) leading to a complete somersault. It is usually introduced as the first rotation as it is an integral part of most entries into water.

The swimmer is taught to attain a back float by moving his head back; as he does so, his feet will move forward and rise to the surface (see photograph 22). If the helper then walks back slowly, the swimmer unwinds from the chair position into a long back float. If the swimmer then brings his head forward, slowly but continuously, until his head is above his feet, he will find that his feet are on the floor. If as he is doing this the swimmer breathes out, it will allow the body to bend more, and if he brings his knees up to his chin while pushing his hands forward (see photograph 23), he will find that in this 'ball' shape it takes much less effort to rotate than in the longer 'stick' position. The helper must allow the swimmer to roll off his supporting hands and resist the great temptation to push the swimmer forward during the recovery.

The ultimate vertical rotation is a somersault, either forward or backward. It is included as a prerequisite to water freedom because the swimmer is thus capable of returning from any position in the water to a safe breathing position whether he is in that position through choice or accident. Teaching this skill is a progression from the basic vertical rotation using the mushroom float as an

22. The back float position. From standing, lay your head back and let your feet come up.

23. The forward recovery; knees up, hands and heads forward ... and *bubbles*. Note the helper is supporting, not pushing.

intermediate stage. The mushroom float introduces the swimmer to a rotation where he becomes submerged. With the swimmer 'sitting in his chair' he is encouraged to push his head back and then to bring his knees up to his chin while supported by the helper. The swimmer then clasps his shins and tucks his head forward. With a controlled rotation the helper allows the swimmer to roll forwards while telling him to hum, thus preventing the water going up his nose. Eventually the swimmer takes up this position himself with no support and is happy to be twisted and turned in all directions knowing that he will always return to this position.

Once the swimmer appreciates the sensation of partially somer-saulting, he is usually more confident in trying a complete somersault alone. This can be achieved in a number of ways. The swimmer can pull himself over the joined hands of two helpers facing each other and then tuck his head in: his momentum should be enough to carry him over and around the arms. Another way is for two helpers to face each other and offer their fists (right/right or left/left) as pivots. The swimmer then places his hands over the fists. Initially the somersault is between the helpers but eventually it is carried out by the swimmer alone. In the early stages an extra person may be required to catch the swimmer as he turns over. This method can be used for forward and backward rolls but at all times the swimmer should be reminded to hum, or gently breathe out.

Forward somersault: keep your head tucked in and ... hummm

LATERAL ROTATION

This rotation is like a rolling log in water and is sometimes called 'horizontal'. Although it can take place in an upright or horizontal position, it is a rotation around the spine. As many disabled people have a tendency to roll, the first stage in teaching the lateral rotation is to teach the ability to correct an unwanted one.

An activity known as 'Don't let me roll you' (see photograph 24) can achieve this well. The helper takes up a position to one side of the floating swimmer at shoulder level. By placing one hand under the nearest shoulder of the swimmer he attempts to roll the swimmer slowly away from him, the other hand being used for support. As the helper lifts and turns the swimmer, the swimmer must turn his head towards the raised shoulder, eventually looking over his shoulder as his body is turned more. This is repeated for the other side. The anti-rotating effect can also be produced by crossing the leg and arm furthest from the turning force over the mid-line of the body towards the side being raised.

At the next stage the swimmer starts the roll himself. This may be

24. Lateral rotation – 'Don't let me roll you'.

25. Lateral rotation – towards the helper.

achieved as described in Rolling around the Circle or as an individual method. The helper stands to one side of the swimmer, supporting him at hip level with one hand out of the water over the swimmer and one below the water underneath. The swimmer can then use any combination of the following to produce a roll towards the helper (see photograph 25): turning his head towards the helper, crossing the far arm and/or leg across the mid-line, shortening the side of the body nearest the helper, twisting the hips or making a slow but continuous reach of the far arm over the near shoulder.

These actions should be enough to produce ¾ roll with little effort. If there is no turning effect, the helper must check that a turning effect due, say, to the head, is not unwittingly being self-corrected by the swimmer twisting his hips in the opposite direction. At about ¾ way through the roll many swimmers will have lost momentum and the roll will tend to 'stick'. This is the time, and not before, to

26. Lateral rotation – a little help at the hip at the half way stage.

complete the roll, if necessary by taking hold of the hips and guiding the swimmer onto his back (see photograph 26). The final part of the roll may be aided by the swimmer straightening the arm that was crossed, away from the side of the body, and pushing slowly towards the pool floor.

A half roll should be practised every time a back float activity comes to the side of the pool. On approach, the swimmer looks to the side in the direction that he is going to roll, and the helper endeavours to position his head on the opposite side. By continuing to look at the side, a roll is initiated that can be easily completed by using the upper arm to take hold of the side; the swimmer's arm takes the 'long way round' (see photograph 29).

27. Lateral rotation – 'You can do this alone but I'm here just in case'.
28. Lateral rotation – unaided!

29. Rotations – this is the right way to come to the poolside.

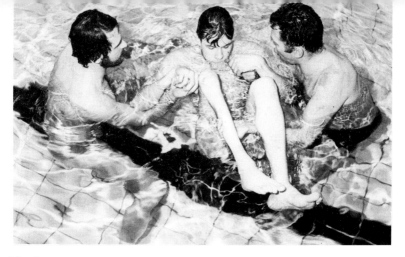

30.   Rotations – preparing for a backward somersault.

COMBINED ROTATIONS

The combined rotation is a vertical rotation forwards, followed by a lateral rotation, so that the swimmer ends up on his back in the safe breathing position. At least one form of this rotation should be taught as early as possible as an effective introduction to the horizontal roll and because it allows the swimmer a 'way out' should he fall on his face.

During a forward recovery (which is a form of vertical rotation), the helper should be directly behind the swimmer as he stands up. If the swimmer should over-recover in this position, he comes directly up against the helper's thighs and hips and so cannot fall forward. If, for some reason, the helper is not in this position, an over-recovery will certainly see the swimmer falling onto his face. At this stage there is no point in trying to heave the swimmer backwards; instead the helper should move further to the swimmer's side. By walking forwards the helper can unwind the swimmer into a long 'stick' shape, face down, which facilitates the ½ lateral roll which follows. The secret of an effective, confident rescue of the situation is to do only one roll at a time before attempting the next; otherwise the helper ends up in a more precarious position as well as being off balance. This should be followed by another forward recovery with the swimmer facing the helper. (It is at such times that helpers can check that the swimmer is happy being submerged and breathes out when underwater. These situations should be rare.)

This activity can be practised by having the swimmer stand up (possibly raising his arms over his head) and then falling forwards. The helper who is standing to one side of the swimmer then asks the swimmer to look at him. Turning the head will automatically result in the shoulders following and the lateral roll is half completed before the swimmer's face is under water. A vertical recovery puts the swimmer's feet on the bottom, but only after he is fully extended in the back float position.

Another example of the combined rotation is a totally unassisted entry into the water. The swimmer sits on the side and places one hand on his knee. The roll entry is more effective if the swimmer then puts his other arm forward at shoulder level and looks over the opposite shoulder. The swimmer then falls forward. The outstretched arm creates drag in the water that is useful so long as the head has produced only a slight rotation of the shoulders. The feet should never be placed in the sluice rail as they may become trapped or used to propel the swimmer over the head of the helper.

For the less advanced, the outstretched arm of the swimmer may be used to guide him into the water during this type of entry. The helper must stand with one shoulder close to the pool-side, the swimmer and helper looking at each other. The helper's arm beside the pool-side guides the far arm of the swimmer, i.e. left to left or right to right arm. The helper must take two large strides towards the pool centre to allow the swimmer to complete a proper rotating entry.

Competence and elegance in rotations is at the core of being water free. Rotations should be mastered and then continually practised, for although it is possible to swim without control of rotation is is not possible to be safe.

31.   Combined rotation – the head leads the way.

Chapter Six
Stage 3: Buoyancy and Upthrust

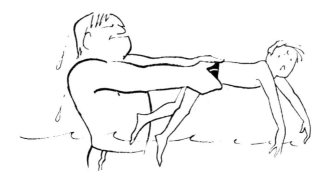

How not to do it: let the water do the supporting

The fact that most people float in water is expressed in this book as 'buoyancy' or 'upthrust'. Buoyancy is the property a body has which enables it to float and upthrust is the force that the water applies to a body. Upthrust is also referred to as a buoyancy force.

Much is talked about confidence with reference to swimming although this is rarely defined precisely, apart from the unhelpful observation that without confidence one cannot swim. Confidence comes from understanding and a sure knowledge of what will happen as a result of certain actions and circumstances. In swimming the belief that the force of upthrust is always acting and will make a body float is probably as close to what people call confidence as one can reach. This belief is based on knowledge and experience which it is the task of the helper to instil using all his skills.

Upthrust can be unmistakably felt if you try to crawl on hands and knees from shallow to deep water. It soon becomes impossible to keep your hands and knees on the bottom as a strong force of upthrust pushes you to the surface.

A *mushroom float* (see photograph 33) is created by curling up into a ball with head tucked in and arms wrapped around your knees. The natural floating position is with the back uppermost, just breaking the surface. If a fellow helper or swimmer pushes you to the bottom or rotates you, upthrust will always turn you and bring you back to the surface, eventually, in the same position. If your swimmer will now allow you to push him to the bottom in a mushroom float this will be an excellent sign of his confidence and appreciation of upthrust.

Try to sit on the bottom of the pool in chest-high water. You will need a very determined effort to get down. The swimmer must jump up, throw his feet forward and with his arms up, attempt to get down far enough to touch bottom. After this has been achieved the swimmer can relax; his feet will drag along the pool bottom as upthrust returns him to a standing position.

An appreciation of upthrust and rhythm will greatly assist the three lifters when making a horizontal lift out of the pool (see p. 24). With careful timing to make the water's upthrust do the work the heaviest swimmer can be lifted onto the poolside with ease. This exercise will show whether helpers are properly adjusted to water.

So again we return to the role of practical experience: this induces confidence, so we relax more; our bodies are less dense and upthrust is more effective.

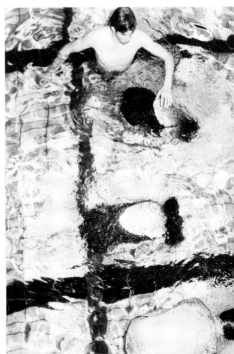

32. Upthrust – this 'bottom walker' is now only just managing to keep his fingers on the tiles.

33. Mushroom floats. All three have been pushed down, now they are bobbing up – that's *upthrust*.

Chapter Seven
Stage 4: Turbulence and Propulsion

Turbulence: the mother duck draws her brood along in her wake

For the keen new swimmer, the propulsive phase is often the first goal but one of the last to be achieved. To have reached this stage safely, the swimmer must go through the previous stages of adjustment to the water, the rotations, and gaining the confidence that water offers great support through upthrust. It is all in the mind; and confidence founded on ability is the paramount factor. This enables the swimmer to relax and thus float. It is the helper's function to generate this confidence, and in order to start he will have to earn the confidence of the swimmer.

The word propulsion is used here because all too often the word 'swimming' is used with the four main swimming strokes in mind. By definition, swimming is progression at or below the surface of the water by working the arms, legs or body. The action of the head must also be included since its corrective effect in balance control is very important.

As the back float gives the swimmer a safe breathing position, it is logical to use this position as a start for any movement. To obtain a similarly balanced position on the front would involve the swimmer's face being in the water. Any action to take a breath would result in disturbance of this balance and the swimmer might become more tense and possibly submerge.

TURBULENT GLIDING

The swimmer is now relaxed and lying on his back; support is given under the centre of gravity. This position is usually between the waist and hips. The ideal point must be found for each swimmer for if the hold is too near the shoulder, the feet will tend to fall. The helper begins to walk slowly backwards, taking the swimmer with him. The hold is gradually relaxed until there is no physical contact. A swimmer at this stage should be able to maintain control and balance. Even though there is no physical contact between swimmer and helper, the turbulent effect produced by the helper's movement results in the swimmer closely following the helper (like ducklings sucked along in the mother's slipstream). This effect is known as *turbulent gliding* and may be made more effective by working the hands backwards and forwards behind and under the swimmer's shoulders to increase suction (see photograph 34).

Sinking as a result of reducing the support of a relaxed swimmer may be due to a number of causes. The most common is incorrect handling. The helper pushes up too hard and tries to do the work of the water, attempting to lift the swimmer higher in the water than is necessary. When the support is reduced, the swimmer sinks to the level to which the water would have taken him originally. If the support is reduced past this level, the body has gained momentum and so tends momentarily to sink further into the water and possibly submerge.

Turbulent gliding: the balanced swimmer moves in the turbulence created by the helper

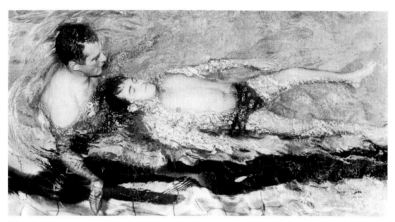

34.   Turbulent gliding – note the turbulence between helper and swimmer. The
swimmer is being 'sucked' into those 'holes' in the water.

Sinking will also result if the swimmer is slightly denser (i.e. thin
and/or heavily muscled) than the supporting water or if in tension.
For these situations the sinking effect may often be overcome by a
faster movement through the water and by using the body shape to
raise the swimmer to the surface. This planing effect can be seen
when a motor boat rises out of the water as it gathers speed; the extra
speed here is produced by the helper walking backwards faster. The
change in shape required is quite small and sinking is commonly
corrected by asking the swimmer to look slightly down towards his
toes. This reduces upthrust at the head and often allows the legs to
rise to the surface. As a result of this the body becomes slightly curved
along all or part of its length, and offers an inclined plane to the water.
When the forces are resolved, there is a small but effective lifting
force acting on the body. Frequently this is the swimmer's first
experience of sustained unsupported movement through the water.
Total disengagement from the swimmer who becomes anxious at the
thought of 'going solo' with a new skill can often be overcome by mild
cunning: the helper can find many other legitimate uses for his hands
– 'Sorry Mary, I've got a fly in my eye'. This is accompanied by careful
disengaging and re-engaging until disengagement is total. Such slight
deception may be all that is necessary to put the swimmer into a
position of independence.

BASIC PROGRESSION — THE FIRST STROKES

After turbulent gliding the next stage is to use the swimmer's own movements to achieve progress. Ideally, the first movements should be created around the centre of gravity so as to minimise the upset to the swimmer's balance. This depends totally on the swimmer's ability or disability, and movement must be achieved by whatever method is available. If possible a *sculling action* is used. This is a hand movement where the hands, palm downwards, are moved to and from the body at the level of the hips rather like the pectoral fins of a fish. Movement here is quite slow and it must be impressed upon the swimmer that it is intended to be just that. Sculling is mainly a balance stroke.

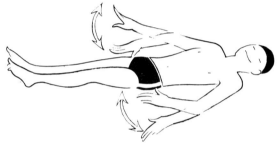

Sculling: the first stage of independent propulsion

Once this is mastered, either leg or further arm action can start. It is unwise to teach both arm and leg action together as faults are more difficult to detect.

Leg action should already be fairly powerful at this stage as a result of speedboat games. The action should start slowly as it then produces less turbulence which can reduce water upthrust. The main faults in the leg action are bending the leg excessively, thrashing, and allowing the hips to fall to a lower level, with the body bent to almost a right-angle. Such bad leg action with bent knees can result in turbulence which produces movement downwards and even backwards. The first two faults can only be remedied by constant reminders to the swimmer to straighten the leg or slow down the kick rate. Where the hips are sinking, the swimmer must be told to raise them by trying to depress the neck and shoulders; even though this will momentarily produce a body extension and increased body tension.

The arm action initially taught is an extended sculling action with both arms together, which is then developed until the arms can be raised just out of the water and taken to the level of the shoulders. At this stage the arms should not make a longer stroke as the body is more unstable when the arms are out of the water. Moreover, the increase in power and pull would not be of any great benefit to the novice swimmer. When the arms are at shoulder level, they enter the water and the swimmer makes a pull quickly to bring the straight arms back to the side of the body; then the cycle is repeated.

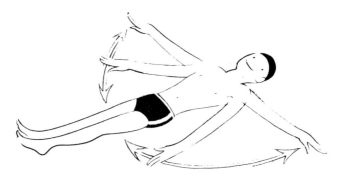

Propulsion: the next stage after sculling

Once the separate arm and leg actions have been mastered, the two are combined. It is then up to the swimmer, under the guidance of the helper, to decide whether to cultivate the arms or legs for the main propulsive force. Many physical handicaps make this decision unnecessary.

STROKE STYLE

Although we initially teach swimming on the back, swimming on the front is not discouraged once the swimmer is fully confident and water happy. Every club should have someone who is capable of analysing a swimmer's method of swimming in order to reduce any wasteful or inefficient styles and allow full development of potential.

Chapter Eight
Physics

Like it or not, it will govern all you do in water

INTRODUCTION

While it is possible to be an adequate helper without a formal knowledge of physics, helpers will eventually find themselves limited unless they acquire sufficient understanding of the action and interaction of water on a body. This chapter falls into two parts: the first sets out and explains the terminology and describes the basic mechanisms and forces; the second examines how the forces are generated and interact. A recurring phrase is 'may be thought of as'. This is used to emphasise that what follows is only one path towards understanding, and there are many others. The one described here is offered as being generally acceptable and reliable. We hope that those who fear science will find this chapter comforting and those who find science boring may discover life added to the dry bones of science taught at school. For whether you understand it or not, the laws of physics discussed in this chapter will govern all you do in the water.

WATER IS DIFFERENT FROM AIR

There are many differences between our everyday world of air and solid surfaces and the world of water. Some are straightforward –

Air is much less dense than water ...

water is wet, air is not; we can feel water; we do not usually feel air.

Two other things become noticeable on entering a pool. First, it is harder to walk or swing one's arms. Many of the movements that are easy to perform in air can only be made slowly in water. Then, going deeper into the pool, an upthrust or lifting – usually called buoyancy – becomes apparent.

It is not only more difficult to move in water, it is more difficult to stop moving or change direction. Try walking for ten paces or so in

... Water is much more dense than air

water that is chest deep, then turn round and walk back: the first few returning steps are very hard going. This is because the water, which is heavy in comparison to air, is now moving. Walking back is like walking upstream in a flowing river.

So, being in water is vastly different to being in air. We must re-learn how to balance, turn, lie down, get up, etc., for the methods for doing these will be different. Many of our ways of doing things on dry land will let us down when we are in the water. This point is of particular significance for the physically disabled who often have little enough confidence in land-based activities, and suddenly discover that their hard-won abilities on land are of no use in the water. With skilled teaching, however, these very difficulties can be turned to great advantage. For instance, if you fall over in water it is a waste of time putting your hand out: but you will, however, fall slowly and are unlikely to be hurt.

BASIC PRINCIPLES

To understand basic physical principles, whether on land or in water, you must be conversant with a few salient definitions of frequently-used terms.

A body

Normally a 'body' is taken to mean a human body. Here, however, any object is considered to be a body. Initially we will explain the principles involved, using solid objects as examples, and in the second part show how the swimmer can teach his body to make use of these. A body has 'properties'. These are characteristics attributable to the body, and are used to describe it. The most commonly used properties are the size and the weight of the body.

Centre of gravity

Our experience of everyday objects shows us that their weight is not evenly distributed. Sometimes the body feels 'off centre' because the weight is not where we expect it to be. We can relate this change in weight to the centre of gravity. The centre of gravity is a point at which all the weight of the body can be thought to be concentrated.

Consider balancing an object such as a symmetrical plank of wood. This is a uniform body which clearly balances at its middle point. You

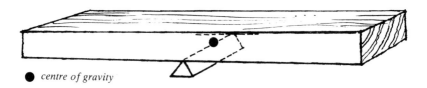

● *centre of gravity*

may turn the plank around, on edge, or even on its end and the plank will always balance on a point below its centre. In this case the centre of the plank is at the centre of gravity. A tin of treacle, however, has its centre of gravity at the bottom in the first illustration below; lay it on its side and pick it up again, and the centre of gravity will have moved.

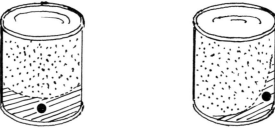

Take a ball: the centre of gravity is usually at its centre. Whichever way the ball is turned, the point on which the ball will balance will be vertically below its centre. Consider a crescent shape or an annulus (like a mint with a hole). The centre of gravity of these shapes does not lie inside the body.

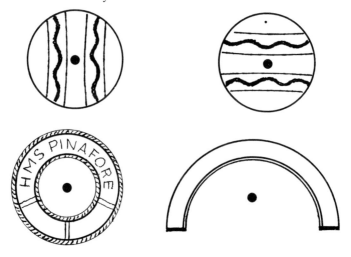

Forces applied to a body may be supposed to act about its centre of gravity. This means that we do not need to know the shape of a body to predict how it will move when it is influenced by a force, provided that we know its mass and where its centre of gravity lies relative to the force. A body in free flight, for example a stick which has been thrown, will rotate freely about its centre of gravity. Think about the child's beach ball which wobbles when pushed instead of rolling. These objects have a centre of gravity which is not at the centre of the ball; it is weighted asymmetrically.

Force

Most of us have an idea of what a force is and understand it to be associated with movement or change. The forces which we discuss here are concerned with movement or the tendency of bodies to move.

A force is described by Isaac Newton's First Law which states:

> A Force is that which changes, or tends to change, a body's state of rest or its uniform motion in a straight line.

The first part is straightforward and simply means that if a body is stationary and then begins to move, a force must have caused this to happen. The second part is a little more complicated as we are used to seeing things slow down and come to rest: it tells us that there is a force responsible for this slowing down – friction.

If a man pushes a car he is applying a force in order to make it move. It will continue to move after he has stopped pushing – until another force brings it to rest. The car will eventually slow down

without hitting anything because of friction. Friction is all around us to an extent that it makes it hard to imagine a world without it. Friction enables us to walk, drive a car, grip objects and use screws to hold shelves up. Whenever a body is seen to change direction, slow down or speed up, there is a force causing this.

Another common experience is related to solid surfaces. We live in a world of hard objects; tables, floors, walls, cups, pencils, books and so on. We are used to these being rigid – if I lean on a wall or sit on a chair, I do not expect either to move. The harder I push, the harder they push back.

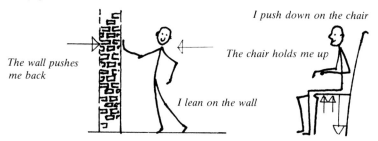

Forces in line and out of line
Forces out of line cause *turning*.

The words moment, couple or torque may be familiar to some readers as being concerned with the turning effect of forces.

Take a ruler and lay it on the table. Push it along the table with one finger so that the line of action passes through the centre of gravity. If you get it just right, the ruler will slide without turning. Now move your finger a little to one side and push; the ruler will turn. The effect is the same if a push is applied on each side of the ruler.

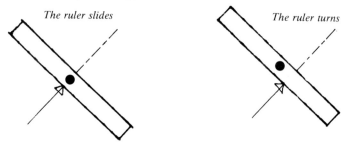

Forces which are not in line cause turning until they are in line

Forces out of line cause rotations

Forces out of line are to be found wherever there is turning or a tendency to turn. This turning is called rotation and is very important in water. Having found out why bodies rotate we need to know how far they turn. There are two cases we need to consider: first, when the forces are removed after rotation has started; second when forces are continuously applied.

1. If we start something turning, such as a bicycle wheel, and leave it to continue, it will eventually be brought to rest by friction. This can be explained by Newton's law even though the motion is rotational.

2. The case when the forces are not removed can be shown by the ruler again. Hold each end between thumb and forefinger, with one hand above the other and the ruler upright. Moving the hands outwards will cause the ruler to turn and it will turn until it is in line with the pull.

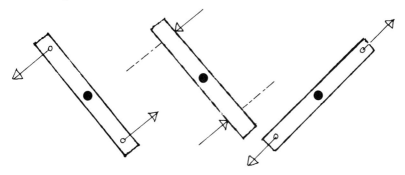

This could have been inferred from the statements above; if the forces out of line cause rotation, and forces in line do not, then rotation will continue until the out-of-line forces are no longer out of line.

Density

Most people have been asked whether it is a pound of lead or a pound of feathers that is heavier, and we all know that they weigh the same. But everyone is tempted to say that the lead is heavier, and generally the statement that 'lead is heavy' is not regarded as silly. Even so, half a pound of lead is clearly only half the weight of a pound of feathers and cannot reasonably be called heavy in comparison.

The significant property here is the *volume* in relation to the *weight*. By volume we mean the space that the body occupies. The volume of a pound of feathers is greater than the volume of a pound of lead. When we say that lead is heavier, we are usually thinking of equal volumes of lead and feathers. This idea of weighing equal volumes is used by engineers and scientists when they talk about density. Lead is more dense than feathers and this is what we mean when we say lead is heavier. Density is measured in units of lb/cubic foot, grams/cubic centimetre, kilograms/litre. Water has a density of 1gm/cubic centimetre, 62.5lb/cubic foot, or 1 kg/litre.

The term 'specific gravity' is used to relate the density of a body to the density of water. It is simply the ratio of the density of the body to the density of water. A body of one cubic centimetre volume weighing 10gm will have a specific gravity of 10, and a body of 50ml volume weighing 100gm will have a specific gravity of 2.

Density = Weight of body ÷ Volume of body
Specific gravity = Density of body ÷ Density of water

One final point about specific gravity. This is also the ratio of the weight of a substance to the weight of an equal volume of water. If we have 1cc of water and 1cc of wood, the water weighs 1gm and the wood weighs 0.75gm (¾gm). The specific gravity of the wood is 0.75. If we take 100cc of each or 100 cubic feet, or any other volume, the wood will always weight ¾ that of the water.

WHY DO WE FLOAT?

Many people claim that they do not float. Usually they are wrong. Surprisingly few cannot float. Floating is dependent on 'density or specific gravity'.

Imagine what it is like to be a block of water in a swimming pool. Consider the shaded block shown below: it has three jobs to do:

1 To sit on the block of water below – 'a'
2 To push apart the blocks at the side – 'b' and 'c'
3 To hold up the block above – 'd'.

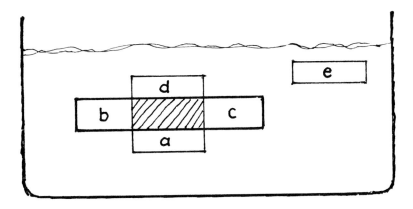

Similarly, 'a' has to hold up 'd' as well as the shaded block and also to rest on the block beneath. The blocks on the bottom or sides of the pool, or on the surface of the water, have slightly different jobs to do as they have the tiles to rest against (in the case of those near the surface, the air).

Obviously water is not made up of separate blocks, and all these examples are merely to help our thinking. We can, however, imagine the blocks to be as large or as small as we like. By thinking of blocks as small grains of sand or salt we begin to see that the sand behaves somewhat like water and the idea is not far from what actually happens in water.

Suppose that somehow we remove block 'd' and replace it with block 'e' which is the same size and weight. The shaded block would be unable to tell the difference and would support whatever we placed there: it would float.

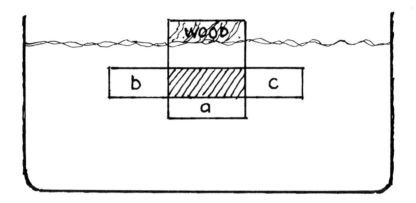

If we then replace block 'd' with a block of wood that still weighs the same as block 'd' but is taller, the shaded block of water will still support the wood since it can only feel its weight, not its volume.

If we now place a weight on top of the block of wood, the layer of water supporting it will experience an increase in weight. This change in circumstances causes the layer to cease support and flow out of the way, allowing the wood to sink a little. The wood will continue to sink until it reaches a level in the water which will support the extra weight. As explained above, block 'a' is supporting both the shaded block and block 'd', and thus supports a greater weight than the shaded block, and the block below 'a' supports all the blocks above it (not unlike cans stacked in a supermarket). This is easily illustrated by floating a block of wood in a bowl of still water, marking the level of the water on the block, and then placing a weight on the wood above its centre of gravity. It will sink a little. (If you try this and your block turns over, do not despair. The reasons for this are explained in the section on 'metacentre' on p. 64).

In all cases so far, the block of wood has remained floating and we have always been able to find a level in the water capable of supporting the weight. The floating block has displaced water, that is to say in floating the block we have pushed water out of the way and replaced it with wood. We have noted that the water displaced by the wood when it floats has the same weight as the wood (this is how the level at which a body floats is determined). Increasing the weight caused more water to be displaced as the block floated lower down. The weight of this extra water displaced by adding the weight to the block of wood is equal to the weight added to the wood. To test this in practice, fill a bowl to the rim with water and gently lower a block of wood into it.

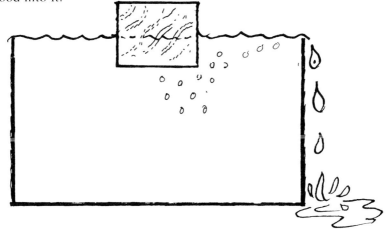

This is an example of Archimedes' Principle, which states that when a body is immersed in a fluid (wholly or partially) it experiences an upthrust or buoyancy force. The magnitude of this force is equal to the weight of the fluid displaced.

If we remember that specific gravity is the ratio of weights for the same volume, it is now possible to devise a simple rule for objects that float. If a body can displace a weight of water greater than its own weight when it is just submerged (i.e. displacing a volume of water equal to its own volume), then it will float. Put another way, in order to float, the specific gravity of a body must be less than 1 – that is, its density must be less than that of water). Human bodies are generally in the range of specific gravity 0.93 – 1.0 (a very few are over 1). This has two results. First, since their specific gravity is less than 1, most people float. Second, since their specific gravity is close to 1, human bodies only *just* float. This is important, for it means that *very small changes* of our bodies will produce dramatic effects in the water. As we only just float, we can have great control over what happens to us in the water.

To complete the discussion, look at what happens when bodies sink. Imagine trying to float a solid block of steel. The block will sink,

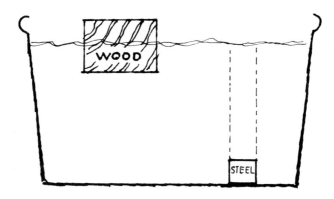

trying to find a layer of water capable of supporting its weight. The water will close over the top of the block and the block will now be displacing the maximum possible volume of water. The buoyancy force will still not be enough to support the weight of the block. The block will continue to sink, descending to a level where the layers of water can support its weight. However, there is now in addition a column of water above requiring support. In other words, there is no level where the block will achieve equilibrium until it reaches the bottom. The specific gravity of steel is much greater than that of water and it can never displace sufficient water to equal its own weight.

CENTRE OF BUOYANCY

When a body floats in water it displaces a volume of water whose weight is equal to its own weight. This water has a shape and weight; we are again thinking about blocks of water. This block of water therefore has a centre of gravity of its own in much the same way as the solid objects discussed at the beginning of the chapter. This point is called the centre of buoyancy. It is of course impossible to do the same sort of balancing experiments to find it and the position must be inferred from our knowledge gained by thinking about solid objects.

In much the same way as a body's weight may be thought of as acting at its centre of gravity, the upthrust or buoyancy force may be thought of as acting at the centre of buoyancy. Water is displaced by the block when it floats: the centre of buoyancy of a body is simply the centre of gravity of the water displaced by the body.

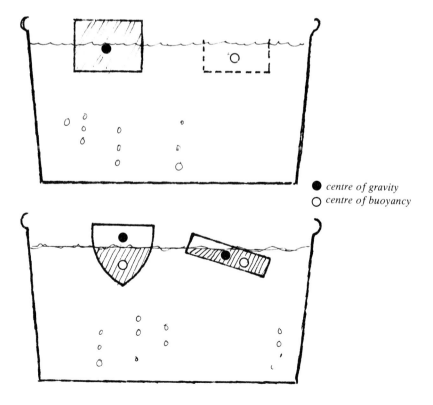

● *centre of gravity*
○ *centre of buoyancy*

WHY ROTATIONS ARE SO IMPORTANT

We have already said that if you put your hand out while in water to prevent a fall, the water will move out of the way and let you fall. Excluding the bottom of the pool, this means that there are no solid surfaces that we can use to give the sort of reaction force we are used to on land (the feel of a solid surface). Everyday movements that you make – walking, stopping, turning round, lying down – all involve using solid surfaces to give a reaction. This is not possible in water and we must therefore re-think how we achieve basic movements in water.

The most basic movements in water are rotations. By rotation a swimmer can get into any position in the water. Clearly a very important rotation is from face down under the water to a safe breathing position. It is also important to be able to move from a floating to an upright position, or from an upright position to a back float. None of these rotations involves a move to another part of the pool. They are all simply rotations about our centre of gravity. As mentioned above, a body in free flight will rotate about its centre of gravity. Forces that are out of line acting on a body will make the body rotate until they are in line. A body in water has firstly its weight acting downwards (and this can be thought of as a single force at the centre of gravity), and secondly because it is floating it has a buoyancy force acting upwards on it. This force is also called upthrust. Any body in water (floating or sinking) has these forces acting upon it.

A block of wood at rest (not rotating) in water must have these forces in line, as shown earlier. Moving the block to put these forces out of line, for example, by pushing down one end and then releasing, will cause the block to rotate until the forces are in line again. Sometimes a body will not return to its original stable position but will continue to roll until it finds a new stable position.

METACENTRE

In water when bodies are moved from a stable position they will roll, sometimes back to the original position and sometimes to a new stable position. We need to find a simple rule which will allow us to decide which will happen. The same rule will explain why a pencil-shaped object cannot be made to float upright and why standing up in a canoe invites disaster.

Let us start by finding out why long thin blocks of wood will float only on their long sides. The two blocks shown below weigh the same and are made of the same material; only their shape is different. They will both float with half their volume under water. Gravity forces act

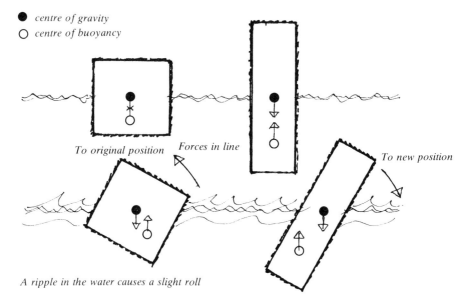

● *centre of gravity*
○ *centre of buoyancy*

To original position *Forces in line* *To new position*

A ripple in the water causes a slight roll

down, buoyancy forces act up and both are in line; there is no rotation. But what happens if the water is gently disturbed? The blocks will be moved out of balance. They will behave differently from each other. Their centres of gravity are fixed points within the body and moving the body does not change the position of this in the body. What does change is the shape of the displaced water and therefore the centre of buoyancy: see how the out of line forces cause different effects.

To determine which way the blocks will roll, a pointer needs to be attached to each block. This is like the mast on a ship and passes through its centre of gravity. As the block rolls, so does the mast. A vertical line drawn through the centre of buoyancy will meet the

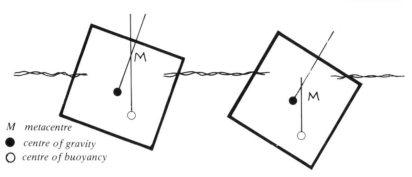

M   metacentre
●   centre of gravity
○   centre of buoyancy

These blocks are stable and have positive metacentres – they will return to upright

pointer at the places marked 'm'. The 'm' points are called the metacentres. The top two diagrams show a block which will roll upright again as the metacentre is above the centre of gravity. The lower left diagram shows a block at the point where a roll is just beginning and the metacentre is in the same place as the centre of gravity. This block is unstable, as the lower right diagram shows. As soon as the roll begins, the metacentre moves below the centre of gravity and the out of line forces act so as to continue the roll rather than return the block to upright.

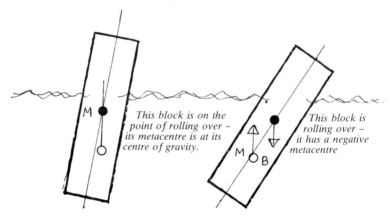

This block is on the point of rolling over – its metacentre is at its centre of gravity.

This block is rolling over – it has a negative metacentre

If the metacentre is above the centre of gravity the body will return to its original position. If the metacentre is below the centre of gravity, the body will roll. The shape of the displaced water causes the

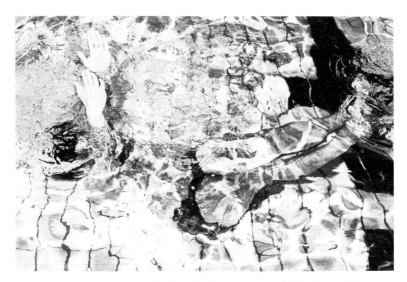

35.   Metacentre – lie on your back and raise your arms; this is what will happen!

centre of buoyancy to move and this moves the metacentre. When the metacentre is at the centre of gravity the body is just balanced (like a pencil on end) and the slightest movement will cause a roll. This is the point of no return.

Metacentre is a difficult concept to grasp. If you are not sure, it is worth drawing a few diagrams yourself so it begins to make sense. Here is a brief résumé.

The procedure to decide whether a body will roll or return upright is as follows:
1. Locate the centre of gravity.
2. Look at the shape of the displaced water.
3. Draw or imagine a pointer that passes through the centre of gravity and is vertical when the body is upright.
4. Draw a vertical line through the centre of buoyancy. The point where these lines cross is the metacentre.

If the metacentre is above the centre of gravity the body is stable and will return upright. If the metacentre is below the centre of gravity the body is unstable and will roll to a new stable position.

So far we have not allowed the centre of gravity to move; it has been a fixed point in the body. Look at the man in the canoe in the

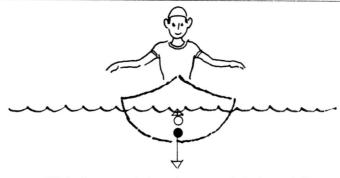

diagrams. With the man sitting, the canoe is balanced. By standing up he raises his centre of gravity. He and the canoe still weigh the same and therefore displace the same amount of water and the forces

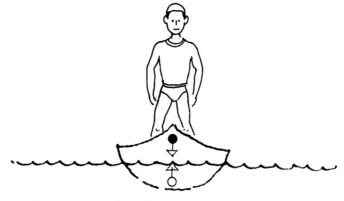

are still in line – just; but his centre of gravity is now above the metacentre and the canoe becomes unstable after a very small roll.

The sudden loss of ships in Arctic waters can be caused by ice forming on the rigging. The extra weight raises the centre of gravity and a rapid roll follows.

The study of metacentre is vital in ship design. Take a passenger liner: the vessel must be capable of returning upright after all the passengers have rushed to one side to see something of interest. A yacht must return upright after a strong wind on the sail. In yacht design a lead keel is used deliberately to lower the centre of gravity.

UPTHRUST

Although much has been said about centres of buoyancy and gravity, always remember that these are only an aid to our thinking. If something is floating in water, it is supported all over the surface that is in contact with the water.

A human body has arms, legs, trunk, and head, all supported by the water. If an arm is lifted out of the water then the water can no longer support it since there is no longer any contact between the two, and the body becomes less stable. If support is removed from one side a roll will occur (see diagram). The situation can be explained either by

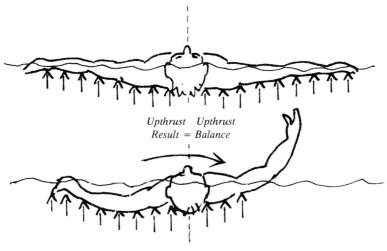

Upthrust   Upthrust
Result = Balance

Upthrust   Reduced upthrust
Result = Roll until balance is restored

a change in the centre of buoyancy or by the upthrust pattern being out of equilibrium. The concept of water being made up of many tiny blocks can again be useful as each block of water will have a small area of body resting upon it. These can only support the body where the two are in contact.

Consider what happens if the water immediately under a body is moved out of position. Water will not tolerate a vacuum, although holes can exist for a short time. The water around the hole will rush in to fill the gap. Some of the surrounding water is supporting the floating body and here there is no water to help fill in the gap. The body is therefore treated as water, and falls into the hole as if it were indeed water.

The block shown below with water being moved from under it by hand will sink slightly or experience a reduction of upthrust as the water is removed. This reduction in upthrust will be seen as the body floating lower in the water. Immediately after the water ceases moving under the body, it will return to its normal floating position.

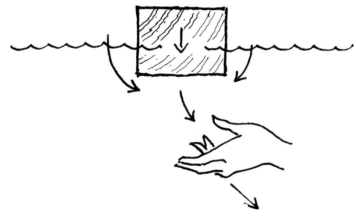

The word used to describe the effect of moving or removing water is *turbulence*. Those familiar with turbulence will realise that the water in a swimming pool is always turbulent and the effect is really due to flow velocity. (The effects of flow velocity were described by Daniel Bernoulli [1700-1782] in his famous equation.) 'Turbulence' is descriptive and convenient and will be used in this book instead of 'flow velocity'.

36. Turbulence – the plastic ball sinks into the 'hole' created by the swishing hands.

TURBULENCE

Turbulence can be looked upon as something that happens independently of all the other effects we have discussed. Although it may change the outcome of all the other forces, it does not interact in the same way.

The simple act of moving water with a hand will cause a reduction in upthrust. This can be seen with anything which has a specific gravity close to 1. Many plastics are useful here: coffee jar lids for example, or lightweight plastic balls with holes in them. Just float one

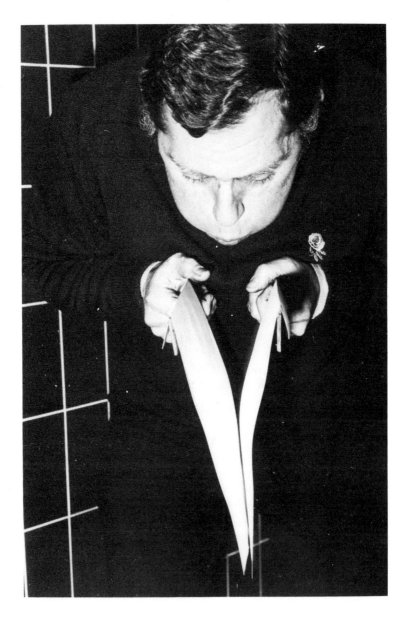

37.   Turbulence – try it; it works.

on the surface of the water and cause turbulence below it by pulling handfuls of water from under it fairly quickly with a cupped hand. It will sink.

Turbulence will work in all directions – up, down, sideways and along the surface of the water. Simply think about making a hole in the water by scooping it away with a cupped hand. Examples of turbulence at work surround us but often go unnoticed. Slip-streaming behind a moving vehicle is making use of a turbulent effect. A simple experiment illustrates what happens. Take a coin and a piece of paper smaller than the coin. Hold one in each hand and let them fall to the floor. The coin falls much faster than the paper. Now put the paper on top of the coin and let them fall to the floor. They will fall at the same speed. The coin is pushing the air away and causing a low pressure region behind it – a hole – and the air, by rushing in to fill the hole, pushes the paper onto the coin. Mother ducks make excellent use of turbulence by gathering up their young and containing them in the turbulent region behind them as they move along. And cricketers bowl 'swingers' by using turbulence.

Turbulence, then, is simply the reduction in pressure, or upthrust in the special case of floating, by a fluid in motion. This can be dramatically illustrated by another simple experiment (see photograph 37). Take two strips of paper about 20cm long and 2cm wide. Fold the top 5cm and hook them each over a pencil as shown. Gently blow between them and they will move inwards. There is a flow of air down the middle creating low pressures, with higher pressure on the outsides where the air is not moving. The high pressure makes the papers move together.

Chapter Nine
Disabilities

This is not a medical student's manual, but its understanding should help to minimise dangers to disabled people and generate a greater appreciation of their problems.

MEDICAL CERTIFICATE

The need for a medical certificate prior to joining an A.S.T. club has been stressed. But it is helpful if, in addition, the doctor includes details of secondary conditions (fits, diabetes, heart trouble, etc.) to ensure the swimmer's safety in the water.

ANATOMY

Only a little knowledge of anatomy is assumed; indeed a detailed knowledge is not required. It is important to know that the body has a bony framework. Bones are connected together by joints which are controlled by muscles and held together by ligaments. In normal conditions, the muscles are in a state of tone or partially prepared for movement. Each muscle is made up of many small muscle fibres which are supplied with blood from the heart via blood vessels (arteries, capillaries and veins).

Nerves from the brain transmit nerve impulses (small electric discharges) to the muscles. Paralysis of the muscles may result if the nerve or brain is damaged. This may take one of two forms, a floppy (flaccid) state or a tense (stiff) state, depending on where the damage has occurred.

ABILITY, NOT DISABILITY

Our philosophy is to stress ability, not disability. It is more important to know how the swimmer's physical shape will react in the water than to have a precise knowledge of his medical handicap.

In the water, the swimmer is naturally supported by upthrust and so enjoys freedom from the artificial aids he may need on land. The use of flotation aids (inflated rings, floats etc.) should be discouraged, for they prolong the journey to being water free and create further balance problems when removed.

Water only reacts to two factors: density and shape. Physical handicaps can thus be divided into two categories: those where the body's density or its shape has a major effect.

Natural floaters

This group comprises swimmers (disabled or not) whose density is relatively less than water, e.g.:

a. Overweight.
b. Those who have wasted, floppy limbs (e.g. caused by muscular dystrophy, spina bifida); paralysed limbs following a fracture of the spine (paraplegia); small compact swimmers with short arms and legs (dwarfs).

The great anxiety of the natural floaters is not that of sinking but that of regaining the upright position from a back float position.

Natural sinkers

These include:

a. Cerebral palsy, either the stiff or wriggly types; those that have sudden uncontrolled movement of limbs or tensing of muscles.
b. Multiple sclerosis.
c. Brain-damaged people following injury, stroke or tumour.
d. Very bony or well-muscled people.

Natural rollers

This group includes any condition which makes the body uneven in shape and with unnatural density distribution:

a. Amputees.
b. Congenitally missing limbs.
c. Hemiplegics who have one side of their body paralysed.

PROBLEMS OF DISABLED PEOPLE

In addition to any obvious handicap, these may include the following:
Acute fear of falling
Difficulty in making themselves understood
Lopsided (asymmetric) body
Difficulty in making movements
Inability to control movement
Poor circulation and breathing capacity
Easily damaged skin, bones and joints
Lack of understanding of the spoken word
Incontinence (lack of control of urine flow and bowel function)
The first visit to the swimming pool is often an emotional time. This may take the form of anxiety, excitement or aggression – so you must expect laughter or/and tears. This is particularly so for the hyperactive and mentally retarded.

COMMON PHYSICAL DISABILITIES

It is very important for helpers to understand the disabilities from which their swimmers suffer, so as to be aware of special dangers and to offer maximum support – emotional as well as physical – when needed. The most common disabilities and suggestions on how to obtain the best and safest results for swimmers with these particular problems are given below.
Handicaps are found in two forms:
a. *Congenital* – where the problem has been present from birth.
b. *Acquired* – may have been caused by accident, disease or old age.

Absent limbs
Although limbs may be congenitally absent from natural causes, certain drugs taken during the mother's pregnancy are known to induce this defect. In the early 1960s some children were born without, or with only rudimentary, limbs, following the use of the drug Thalidomide. Their limitations are the physical ones of their limbs and particular care is needed in diving where there are no arms to protect the head on entry into the water.

Achondroplasia or 'dwarfism'

These have large heads (but not 'water on the brain') and short arms and legs. A point to note is that they may also have impaired hearing.

Amputees

Amputation may be of arms or legs, partial or complete; the majority occur in the lower limbs. Special care on the poolside is required, so use ambulance chairs or 'transit seats' and keep artificial limbs dry and near the poolside. Ensure the skin is dry before fitting the limb. The poolside is very dangerous for people using aids – rubber ferrules may slip on the wet surface.

Amputees, once balanced in the water, can become very strong swimmers. If the amputation is due to an operation because of diabetic or circulatory problem, extra care must be taken of the skin.

Arthritis

This involves swelling, stiffness and pain in the joints. In rheumatoid arthritis there is generalised swelling of many joints, particularly starting in the hands and feet. This is often associated with poor health.

Asthma

Allergy plays a large part in causing this condition and the consequent difficulty in breathing can cause problems. Do not push asthmatics into competitive swimming unless they genuinely wish to compete. Watch they do not become over-tired or stand around getting cold.

Brain damage

This may result from an injury at birth, a road accident, or brain tumour causing hemiplegia, physical or mental handicap, and possibly giving rise to visual or hearing problems. Many brain-damaged people are hyperactive and have great difficulty in co-ordination and concentration.

Cerebral palsy or 'spastics'

A condition resulting from damage to the brain. This is sometimes accompanied by mental retardation, epilepsy, and emotional disorders. There are three main types of cerebral palsy:

Athetoid: This is marked by uncoordinated, involuntary movement, resulting often in writhing, wriggling limbs. It is often accompanied by poor head control and considerable difficulties with speech and swallowing. Efforts to control movement cause grimacing and increased movement.

Spastic: Muscle spasm and jerky movements, often with rigidity. The swimmer may suffer from paralysis of the body down one side (hemiplegia) or of all four limbs (tetraplegia) to a greater or lesser degree. The arms are often held bent up close to the body and the legs stretched out or crossed in a scissor position. The circulation is poor because of rigidity; speech can be impaired.

Ataxic: This is characterised by the inability to make rapid co-ordinated movements and a staggering gait.

Participation in swimming obviously depends on the degree of disability, and all cases of cerebral palsy have balance problems. 'Spastics' easily choke and often have difficulty in closing their mouths; swallowing water leads to vomiting. They are excitable and not aware of their own limitations. Many with cerebral palsy enjoy and benefit from the relative relaxation of muscle spasm which occurs during swimming sessions. If they can swim, they improve control, speed and stroke the longer they are in the water, and are better in long rather than short races. On the poolside, they may be able to walk – with almost a drunken sort of gait – with an aid or holding on to someone, or they may be chairbound. They are aware of when and where they need help. Give them time to adjust and do not take away their independence by rushing to their aid. Many spastics have impaired hearing and considerable visual problems and may suffer from fits.

Cystic fibrosis

This is a hereditary disease which affects the pancreas and gives rise to poor absorption of food. These swimmers suffer with chronic chest infections.

Diabetes

In this condition the pancreas is not functioning adequately and the body cannot control the level of blood sugar. Many are overweight and suffer from arthritic joints, especially hips, knees and ankles. The circulation may be affected and this gives rise to increasing problems with sight, skin infections and ulceration; in serious conditions amputation of limbs may be needed to prevent the spread of gangrene.

Dislocated hips

Children may be born with dislocated hips or may develop a conditions known as 'Perthes disease' (a condition caused by fragmentation of the head of the femur or thigh bone). Both may be treated with splints and during this time the child must not be allowed to take his weight on the affected side.

Epilepsy

The question of whether people with epilepsy should swim has for many years aroused controversy, not least among members of the medical profession, and the National Co-ordinating Committee on Swimming for the Disabled, in conjunction with the British Epilepsy Association, has produced a special leaflet called *Swimming and Epilepsy*. An epileptic attack is due to an occasional sudden abnormal discharge from the brain cells. Epilepsy itself is an established tendency to recurring fits. Anyone can have a fit if the insult or stress to the brain is great enough. This occurs in people of all ages, social backgrounds and levels of intellect.

There are three main types of attack:

Grand mal (or convulsive fits): Here the epileptic holds his breath, his limbs go into spasm and unconsciousness occurs. After the attack convulsive movements occur and the epileptic may appear confused or tired for some time.

Petit mal: A single short period of vagueness with loss of comprehension. This attack may be repeated.

Psychomotor fits: These vary a great deal but often consist of automatic actions associated with clouding of consciousness. The person appears to be conscious but is unable to respond during the attack.

All epileptic swimmers must be watched whilst they are in the club and appropriate action taken if a fit occurs in or out of the water.

First aid for epileptic fits

Keep calm; you cannot stop a fit once it has started. Ease the person to the floor and loosen any tight clothing. Prevent him from hurting himself on furniture or the poolside. Turn him on his side so that the saliva runs out of the mouth: do not attempt to insert anything between his teeth. As the fit subsides the person will be exhausted, so allow him to sleep if he wishes.

Fragilitis ossium or osteogenesis imperfecta ('brittle bones')

The people with this condition are small and their limbs are deformed by frequent fractures. Deafness can be an associated disability. Great care should be taken on the side of the pool and when entering or leaving the water.

Haemophilia

This is a congenital condition, mainly in males, where a minor injury causes excessive bruising; bleeding into joints causes pain, swelling and stiffness, and may lead to an arthritic condition. Haemophiliacs should swim only in controlled conditions and care must be taken to ensure that they do not bang or bump their bodies either in the water or on the poolside. Handling must never be rough or too firm.

Hydrocephalus

An enlargement of the head due to excess fluid round the brain tissue which is often associated with spina bifida. Where a valve has been inserted to control the condition care should be taken in the handling of the head and neck, especially as the swimmer gets into and out of the pool.

Multiple fractures

See rehabilitation

Multiple sclerosis or disseminated sclerosis

A progressive condition where isolated plaques of degeneration occur throughout the nervous system, producing a variety of signs and symptoms. As paralysis increases the limbs tend to become tight or spastic; there is a loss of sensation and a poor blood circulation.

Incontinence may occur. Vision and speech can be affected. Sometimes people disabled by this condition seem to have more energy and better control of their limbs when in the water. Often they are euphoric. Watch and assist when required, but help them maintain their independence as long as possible. They will get tired quickly and should not be over-stretched. Times in competition swims are very variable and become progressively slower.

Muscular dystrophy

A progressive disease of muscles starting in childhood. There is no neurological deficiency, so great psychological support is necessary. The muscles lose their power and are replaced by fibrous tissue; gradually the paralysed limbs develop deformities of the joints. Owing to inactivity the young person puts on a great deal of weight. The circulation is poor and skin easily damaged. Eventually the respiratory muscles are affected and swimming must be discontinued. Great care is needed, as for multiple sclerosis.

Parkinson's disease

A progressive disease of older people, also known as paralysis agitans because of the constant movement of the hands and feet. The limbs gradually become spastic, balance is affected and the loss of sensation and poor circulation cause problems. Care is similar to that for cerebral palsy.

Poliomyelitis

This is a viral infection attacking the nerve cells of communication between the spinal cord and muscles, resulting in paralysed (weak or floppy) muscles. This paralysis may be an isolated weakness of a shoulder or foot or may be widespread paralysis of a whole limb. If this is so, there may well be deformity of the limb due to muscle wastage and fibrous contractions. Affected limbs have a poor blood supply and skin damage is a considerable hazard. Great care must be taken – as for spina bifida.

Polyneuritis
An infection of the spinal cord producing generalised weakness and flail limbs. Poor circulation and sensory loss allow the skin to be easily damaged. Care as for spina bifida.

Rehabilitation
Swimming after an injury, operation or heart attack can, under controlled conditions, greatly encourage the body to resume normal functioning. Swimming improves the circulation and heart action, improves muscle tone and joint movements and restores morale and self-confidence.

Rubella syndrome
This may affect a child whose mother contracted German measles during pregnancy. Such children are usually under-sized and clumsy in their movements. Co-ordination is not easy and they often suffer from hearing loss. There may also be a congenital heart lesion and/or sight difficulties.

Sensory handicaps
Deafness: Loss of hearing usually makes balance more difficult. As deaf aids cannot be worn in water, many deaf people lip-read and it is possible to communicate by facial expression and hand signs. Deaf children are often compensated by good vision and are excellent mimics.

Visual handicap: There are varying degrees of visual handicaps. Partial sight is quite common in congenital handicaps. Many blind people have excellent hearing and find their way about by vibrations in the air and water. Those who have a detached retina must avoid knocks and strenuous activity, such as diving.

The visually handicapped often have an increased sensitivity to the environment and an extra ability to concentrate, which makes them quick to learn.

Skin problems
Burns or skin grafts may cause tightness and difficulty in moving limbs; but limbs move more freely in water. These swimmers are

often very self-conscious and prefer to be covered with towels if waiting on the bathside.

Psoriasis and eczema are chronic non-infectious skin conditions; they may be affected by chemicals used to purify the water, so take especial notice of any reaction after swimming.

Swimmers who have unhealed skin wounds, boils, varicose ulcers, verrucas, or recent vaccinations, should not swim until the skin is healed. Care must always be taken to ensure that skin lesions do not result from careless handling at swimming sessions.

Spina bifida

A failure in spinal development before birth results in the spine being divided by a cleft – normally the spinal cord is completely protected by a canal of bone. This malformation leads to varying degrees of paralysis of the lower limbs plus hydrocephalus. Hydrocephalus is relieved by a plastic tube containing a valve which drains the fluid from the spaces in the brain into the blood system; the tube usually runs under the skin on the right side of the neck.

Paralysis of the nerve supply to the bladder and bowel may occur, causing incontinence. This is relieved by an artificial opening in the abdominal wall which is connected with a bag. In spina bifida cases bags should be emptied before the swimmer enters the pool. Care must be taken in getting the swimmer out of the pool to make sure that the bag is not squashed or pulled out of position. Meticulous care of the skin is important because of the lack of feeling: the swimmer does not realise that a rough surface will scratch or bruise his limbs or buttocks. Unwary helpers can do real damage which will take months to heal (largely because of the poor blood supply to the skin). A moment of carelessness may cause weeks of unnecessary suffering where the handicapped person is unable to wear shoes/calipers/supports and has to resort to a wheelchair. In the dressing room or on the poolside extra care is needed when handling spina bifida swimmers as the lower limbs are usually very floppy and easily twisted. Most of the swimmers rely on their upper limbs and their arms may become exhausted. Great care must be taken that feet do not trail on the bottom of the pool, or along the ground if the swimmer is in a wheelchair.

Spinal cord paralysis

A disease or accident which affects the part of the body supplied by nerves below the level of the injury. The paralysis may be flaccid (floppy) or spastic (stiff, tight) and affects either the lower limbs (paraplegia) or all four limbs (tetraplegia). If the lesion is in the neck, the limbs and muscles of respiration are affected. Below the lesion there is impaired circulation and sensation so that the skin is easily damaged. Sudden precipitation into cold water may lead to an increase in muscle spasms which could cause problems. Otherwise, the difficulties are similar to those of spina bifida and great care is needed with the paralysed limbs and the skin.

Stroke

This is caused by an interference to the blood supply to part of the brain and frequently affects one side of the body, giving rise to a condition known as hemiplegia. Speech and vision may also be affected. Remember that limbs that are paralysed for any reason have a poor blood supply; this means that the skin is easily damaged, bones are more easily broken and joints dislocated, so especial care must be taken at all times.

COMMON MENTAL DISABILITIES

Autism

This condition produces great problems in communication. Autistic people often flap or clap their hands. Their lack of understanding makes it difficult for them to co-operate, but they respond to repetition of individual activities in the same sequence week after week. Changes in routine may produce severe adverse reaction and have to be carefully introduced.

Children with learning difficulties

These children are often hyperactive or emotionally disturbed. Others have spatial problems with a resulting poor body image. They benefit from working with other children.

Mental retardation

This can take many forms; amongst the commonest and most easily recognised is mongolism – also known as Down's syndrome. Mongol children are late in walking and talking. They have lax joints and often have problems of vision, hearing, a heart lesion, and are prone to chest infections. Their power of concentration is limited and can only be retained for very short periods. Often mongols have no idea of danger. They are well-known extroverts.

Severely subnormal children are able to benefit from movement in water. As water surrounds the swimmer and is in constant motion, it serves as a great stimulus and can result in the swimmer making movements for themselves. Water tends to encourage such children to 'wake up'.

GENERAL

The helper may feel overwhelmed by his lack of knowledge – do not be discouraged. The first and prime requirements are a smile and a genuine enthusiastic wish to help. This attitude will induce 'self-forgetfulness' and a happy and relaxed time can be enjoyed by all.

Maintain eye-to-eye contact with your swimmer; this will enable you to discern if he is happy and becoming more confident. Skilful hands can do a lot of talking too.

Socks and stockings are an excellent way to protect insensitive feet and legs in danger of abrasion.

Chapter Ten
How to Run a Club

The reason for running any club is self-evident – the unity of those with a single purpose, good company and friendship. For disabled people this is all the more important as they tend to be cut off from the hustle-bustle and fun of normal life.

In the water everyone comes closer to equality, and disabled people can enjoy the hurly-burly, organised rough play and games with those more fortunate than themselves. The able-bodied will also find a great deal of enjoyment and fulfilment in their lives from their club membership, not least from the appreciation of their own well-being.

Our club will thus resemble as closely as possible any other club, where members can step outside the possible restrictions of their everyday existence and enjoy a talk, discuss fears and joys, and have fun together.

STARTING A CLUB

The most obvious prerequisite is to establish a sufficient demand. In practice everything tends to start on a small scale and the beginnings of the club may be a few parents who have become friends and wish to teach their disabled children to swim. Once such a group has secured 'pool time' the seed corn of the club has been sown; and with enthusiasm, boundless energy and pertinacity, progress can be made towards the fully-developed club.

All club work is voluntary and a successful club will need many volunteers: administrators, instructors and swimming helpers, transport officer, life savers, bathside organisers, drying and dressing helpers, refreshment providers and a few 'spares' to have a chat with anyone who is new or a bit lonely. So there is room for a wide variety of people to help and their combined enthusiasm will build the club's success.

Word of mouth amongst friends and acquaintances is the best means of swelling numbers but there are several other ways of increasing membership. Write to the editor of the local newspaper and see if you can persuade him to put in an article with photographs, send notices to the local authority social and medical departments, to 'special' schools, physiotherapy departments of local hospitals and other interested bodies. This may well produce a sudden rush and imbalance of swimmers to helpers. Close contact with your nearest existing club will be very helpful in the early days.

AFFILIATION TO THE ASSOCIATION OF SWIMMING THERAPY

It is desirable to seek affiliation to the Association of Swimming Therapy. The clubs in the Association are divided into regions known as A.S.T. Regional Areas (A.S.T.R.A.s). Clubs pay a small affiliation fee, based on the number of members, to the Regions. Regions pay a nominal sum for affiliation to the A.S.T.. More details of the A.S.T. are given in the chapter on training courses, and for further information, contact your Local Regional Secretary, who will, among other things, be able to give information on the important matter of insurance.

SWIMMING POOL

As most pools are owned by the local authority, their co-operation, goodwill and encouragement are vital. Try very hard to establish a regular weekly or fortnightly time for club activity by a careful and organised approach to the relevant town hall authority. Cultivate the interest and respect of the baths staff and try to make sure that the water is kept at a constant 80°. Life savers are absolutely essential. Baths staff or regular members of your local Life Saving Society are best, but in their absence ensure you have two club life savers who should constantly survey the water.

COMMITTEE

Your committee should include: chairman/president, secretary, treasurer, transport organiser, swimmers' and parents' representatives, bathside organiser, chief instructor and competitions organiser. Hold regular meetings to discuss club activities and swimmers' progress. Swimmers' record cards will be invaluable here.

Name	Age	
Address	Date of birth	Photograph

BADGE TESTS	Date	Time	Distance
Red			
Yellow			
Green			
Blue			

The success of the club will reflect the efficiency of the committee members. Make sure proper minutes are maintained and consider appointing a local dignitary as chairman if he is genuinely useful. Don't forget the disabled – who better to run and understand their club! Some A.G.M.s are dull, but if the occasion is enlivened by an annual award and badge test presentations by the mayor, and refreshments, a good attendance is more likely.

One of the first jobs for the committee will be to select a club name, order headed paper and have a badge designed and produced.

The local general practitioners should be informed to enable them to pass this information to schools and other local doctors; in this way young and old can be referred to your club.

38. *(Facing Page)* Safe handling with the aid of local authority transport.

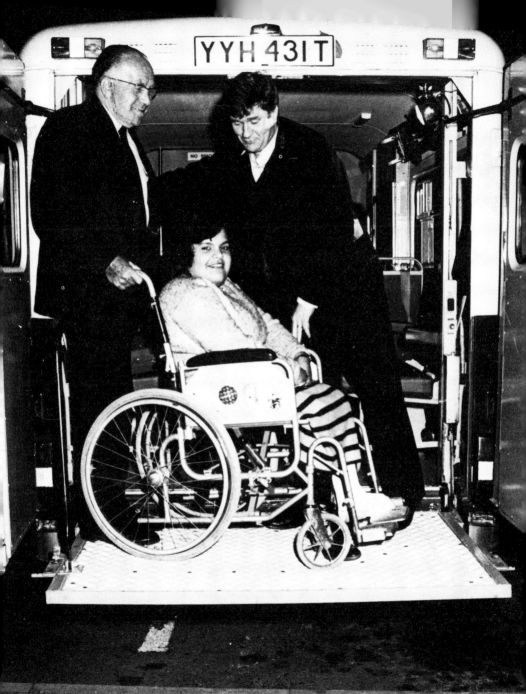

TRANSPORT AND ESCORTS

The efficient and strict management of transport and escorts is another essential lifeline. If club volunteers or helpers from Rotary or other local voluntary organisations are not available then the transport department of the social services must be sought out. The correct approach and a well-conceived plan is vital to obtain their co-operation. Such transport will inevitably involve the local authority in heavy costs and though it should be remembered that they have statutory obligations, nevertheless your plan should try to keep expenditure down as far as possible.

It is normal for a club to provide voluntary escorts who should be responsible and carefully briefed as to their precise duties, and of a friendly disposition; for they will be the swimmers' first club contact.

Escort duties will include:

1. Ensure punctuality on picking up and returning swimmers to their home.
2. Always escort swimmers to and from their front doors and, with the severely and mentally handicapped and children, into the hands of parents or responsible adults.
3. Maintain friendly relations with parents; the escort may be their only club contact.
4. Ensure the safety and comfort of passengers to and from the baths, seeing that all are seated and that wheelchairs are effectively secured.
5. Remember the driver is in sole command: always obey him and never operate the wheelchair lift without his specific instruction.

Without efficient transport your club cannot flourish.

MEMBERSHIP APPLICATION

The form set out opposite contains questions designed to ensure the swimmer's safety, not to exclude him from the club. Warning of epilepsy, for example, must be passed by the bathside organiser to lifeguards and helpers. The importance of the swimmer's medical certificate and the need for the presence of a medically qualified person are self-evident.

APPLICATION FORM

Name of Club...

Address of Club...

Secretary's name and address...

I wish to apply for membership of the above club for disabled
swimmers.

Full name...

Address................... School/workplace...................

               ....

               ....

Telephone number........... Date of birth....................

Have you any of the named problems
      Visual difficulties   Yes/No
      Hearing difficulties   Yes/No
      Fits   Yes/No
      Heart condition   Yes/No
      High blood pressure   Yes/No
      Asthma or Bronchitis   Yes/No
      Nerve or Muscle complications   Yes/No
      Skin problems   Yes/No
      Are you in a wheelchair   Yes/No
      Do you use walking aids   Yes/No
      Any other problem   ....

Do you require any special care/attention prior to entry to
water ....

Signature of parent, guardian or applicant ....

Agreement from medical adviser that the above is correct and
that you may take part in an organised swimming activity.

Signature of doctor...

Address...

Date...............

Whilst the Club is affiliated to the Association of Swimming
Therapy, which is an expert body in the teaching of the
handicapped by the Halliwick Method, we are unable to accept
responsibility for loss or damage to person or belongings.
Members joining must abide by the Rules of the Club.

MEMBERSHIP CARD

It is a good plan to issue a membership card, as set out on the facing page, when subscriptions have been paid, since this instils a sense of belonging. A well-designed lapel badge and tee-shirt are also popular items and help to distinguish different clubs at galas.

A register of attendance should be kept for every swim session and details of any accident that may, despite precautions, occur. A swimmer who fails to attend for several weeks should be visited to see if any help can be given.

NEWSLETTER

This is an excellent way to communicate past and future events. Whilst there is normally one written by the Region there is no reason why the club should not have its own. The chief problem is to find an enthusiastic and energetic editor – a disabled person would be ideal. Initially, production need not be more lavish than duplicated sheets which can be circulated by hand or with other notices through the post.

In any event, support your Regional newsletter with information of your club activities.

SOCIAL ACTIVITIES

Do remember that you are primarily a swimming club and that swimming for disabled people and their safety is your first priority. Your first duty is to the swimmers and your second to the local authority who, at great cost, provide the pool time, staff and transport without which no club could exist. Ensure that you always fulfil those duties and honour the trust placed in you.

However, as numbers increase there will be a natural demand for other activities, and the disabled should be encouraged to suggest and organise these themselves as far as possible. Ideas for these are limitless but experience has shown that the following are popular:
1. Outings to the sea, where additional buoyancy is an advantage.

MEMBERSHIP CARD

front

(CLUB EMBLEM)   SWIMMING   CLUB

Affiliated to the Association of Swimming Therapy

MEMBERSHIP   CARD

SENIOR/JUNIOR

Name ....

Subscription received £.....
Expires: 31 December 19 ...

P.T.O. Club Rules

back

1. Subscriptions for adult swimmers £.........
   Juniors (under ...) £.........

2. Subscriptions are due on 1 January each year.

3. A medical certificate is required from and an
   official application form must be signed by a
   new swimmer or his/her parents.

4. No swimmer is allowed in the pool without per-
   mission from the Chief or Senior Instructor.

5. Only swimmers and official helpers to participate
   in swim sessions.

6. The techniques used are those of the Association
   of Swimming Therapy to which body the club is
   affiliated.

7. All swimmers must remain inside the baths premises
   during sessions and no unauthorised visitors are
   allowed inside except to a gala.

2. Annual or Christmas party with dancing – excellent fun and exercise can be had of the wheelchair variety.
3. Inter-club parties, galas and week-end visits to other clubs.
4. Visits to places of interest and entertainment can often be arranged at favourable admission rates.

FINAL WORDS

Within your club there will be much hidden talent, and disabled members with modern and useful ideas – help them to find, each one, their niche. There is almost no task that the disabled person cannot undertake, from helper in the water to chairman of the committee in administration; their enthusiasm is amazing. Who better to represent the disabled than themselves? The opportunity of responsibility and its successful fulfilment will greatly improve morale and confidence and bring benefits to the disabled in everyday life.

Our insistence that everyone be called by their Christian name is a symbol of the equality that you must strive for. The happiness of your club will be the touchstone of this achievement.

Chapter Eleven
Games

INTRODUCTION

Much of this book is devoted to the practical aspects underlying a basic teaching method. This, however, is not necessarily intended to be presented 'raw' to the swimmer; indeed, few people under instruction will be able to cope with the ideas if taught in this way. What is needed is an effective way of teaching physical ability in a new environment. The answer is to be found by watching children.

Most of our own basic physical abilities are acquired as children by playing, experimenting and learning from each other. This brings us to the idea of games. Once games are made central to activity in water many other benefits flow and several problems disappear. Groups are necessary for most games; this immediately takes pressure off the helper-swimmer relationship: both become members of a group. Copying is easier when swimmers are trying to do the same thing together, in close visual and physical contact. Disengagement from helpers is easier as part of the game and an element of competition is introduced. Continuity is maintained by linking games together and time spent in the water does not become a set of exercises. Songs and chants may be used to pace a game, allowing slow and fast games to be mixed, giving periods of relaxation and others of warming-up activity. Confidence and security depend very much on knowing what to expect; as known old favourites, games facilitate this and their repetition is helpful.

Games are easily related to children but it is wrong to assume that they are the exclusive province of the young. Whilst it would be equally wrong to pretend that learning by games suits everyone, it is important to realise that the benefits which arise make it worth a considerable effort to adapt, invent and devise games for groups of all ages and types.

Games as represented here, then, are to be taken in their widest context of a ritualised interaction limited only by the helper's or swimmer's imagination and due regard to our principles. Your club session will gain extra popularity and life when a game is introduced. Each of the following games has a name. This is important. All games should have names, as this allows everyone involved to understand exactly what is to happen when the game is announced.

In the section on games given below, a set pattern is followed, information being listed under five headings: formation, description, teaching points, checking points, variations. 'Formations' are the key to linking games together to build a programme. (H stands for helper, S for swimmer). 'Teaching points' covers the reasons for each game, and points out what learning should be taking place. 'Checking points' draws attention to other skills (or their absence) that can be observed while the swimmers are concentrating on the current game, so that it can be seen if earlier lessons have really been grasped or are merely performed on demand. Finally, variations are suggested to prevent boredom and encourage development of skills by making the game harder. These games are intended as a basis. They cover a range of abilities, most basic skills, and include slow and fast activities. Helpers who have realised the value of games will soon want to develop the games that follow and add games of their own to the list.

We have placed the games in order of simplicity, though helpers can make each one progressively more difficult.

39.   Two happy groups – but can you spot the handling errors?

1   CANOES — MOTOR BOATS — WRIGGLING

S	S	S	S	S	*poolside*
H	H	H	H	H	

Formation Helpers behind swimmers who face the side of the pool. Swimmers put their heads back (apprehensive swimmers can use the helper's shoulder as a pillow). Helper's hands balance the swimmer's body in the middle of the back (at waist level).

As *canoes* the swimmers are moved through the water by the helpers without any leg or arm movements.

As *motor boats* the hand support is the same but the swimmer provides an engine by splashing legs or pulling with arms (see photograph 40).

When *wriggling* the swimmer does not use arms or legs and should be completely relaxed. The helper's hands are along the side of the swimmer's body at waist level and the swimmer is moved through the water by the helper in large 'S'-shaped curves. The helper should encourage the swimmer to 'look at me' to facilitate the curve, thus underlining the importance of the head in changes of direction.

In each activity the swimmer should be landed at the pool side by half a roll.

Teaching points Head control assists vertical recovery. The swimmer experiences upthrust and turbulence. In wriggling the swimmer helps control his body by turning the head from side to side to look at helper. This is an excellent activity to relax tense swimmers.

Variations:Wriggling round the Rocks (see photograph 41) is similar to wriggling but on a random basis (swimmers not in line) with individual swimmers and helpers.

40. Motor Boats – think of feet as engines in this race.
41. Wriggling round the Rocks – the turn of the head helps restore balance as the swimmer goes round a curve.

2   BICYCLES

poolside

H	H	H	H	H
S	S	S	S	S

Formation Helpers in line, backs against side of pool with swimmers' backs against helpers' chests. Swimmers' flat palms downwards, supported on helpers' flat palms upwards.

Description At 'Go' swimmers cycle from one side of pool to the other. This is excellent for the severely handicapped as the helper can keep maximum control, by pushing up with the palms if the swimmer falls forward or pressing forward with the shoulder if the swimmer falls back. Swimmers should be encouraged by the helper whispering into the swimmer's ear to pedal hard, maintain balance and 'blow bubbles' when face gets near water.

Teaching points Forward recovery, balance, breathing and head control; for helpers, good secure hold.

Checking points (Ensure swimmers' feet do not trail or strike bottom and cause injury). Allow swimmer to find his own point of balance in the water; don't strive to lift him up. Swimmers should grasp the side of the pool with both hands to finish race. The group leader should be in the middle of the line – or, if there are sufficient helpers, in front – so that swimmers can cycle towards him.

Variations Small swimmers or children may grip a helper's upturned thumbs. To encourage disengagement swimmers may face helpers, who provide increasingly less support on outstretched palms. Swimmers may be held at waist level, thus increasing the need for head control, as a more difficult progression.

42. Bicycles – secure back hold through swimmer's arms, with vocal encouragement.

3 POACHED EGGS

poolside

H	H	H	H	H	H
S	S	S	S	S	S

Formation Swimmers in front of helpers, both facing away from the poolside.

Description Swimmers attempt to turn a plastic 'poached egg' (available from the A.S.T.) over as many times as possible while blowing it across the pool.

Teaching points Head and balance control. Breathing control, visual co-ordination and confidence overcoming fear of getting face wet.

Checking points Water adjustment (the swimmer's attitude to being splashed).

Variations 'Blow football', where the swimmer and helper face each other and blow the 'poached egg' between themselves. Swimmer's and helper's hand may be held to form a 'fence' to keep the ball in play.

43. Poached Eggs – blowing the eggs improves breathing control.

4 RAG DOLLS

H S H S H S H S H   *poolside*

Formation Everyone faces the side of the pool, with an extra helper at the end of the line. Helpers' hands are palms up, swimmers' flat with palms down, no gripping.

Description Swimmers move their heads backwards and the toes come to the surface. Helpers walk slowly backwards across pool, swimmers floating on their backs. Before reaching the opposite side of the pool the swimmers are asked to make themselves into a ball. They put their heads forward and allow their bodies to trail behind, floating on their stomachs as the helper walks forward to the starting point (see photograph 44). This is repeated a number of times back and forth across the pool.

Teaching points Head control. Balance of body in water.

Checking points Holding positions. Blowing bubbles into the water when moving forward. Adjustment – balance in water. Vertical rotation.

Variations With the young and nervous swimmer the hold may be a short arm hold (see photograph 45) which will progress to the arm at full length. It is possible to use the line formation for walking, jumping and bicycling across the pool.

44. Rag Dolls – with short arm hold and legs trailing behind.
45. Rag Dolls – with short arm hold. Look at the ceiling please, not at the camera!

5 SNAKE

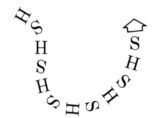

Formation Alternate swimmer and helper in a line. This can start at the side of the pool with everyone's hands on the side; then turn right and link up with the swimmers' arms round helpers' waists. To secure the more disabled swimmers, helpers' arms should form a box by hands firmly holding the waist of the helper in front.

Description With the most competent swimmer in the lead, the snake moves forward. Everyone should have feet on the ground and take little steps forward, leaning away from the head of the snake which is trying to catch its tail – the last swimmer at the end of the line. Forward progress is important; watch the leader so as to lean away from the direction he is taking to prevent the tail of your snake being caught. Change swimmers so all swimmers have a chance to lead the snake.

Teaching points Head control; note that the first way you change direction is by moving your head that way. 'Blow bubbles' when swimmer's face gets near water. Encourage swimmers to keep low in water to experience upthrust and increase their stability, feeling also the surge of the swirling water as the snake twists.

Checking points Ensure inert feet do not scrape on bottom and that everyone holds tight.

Variations Allow snake head to grip tail and form circle – helpers raise inside arm, slide it down to form circle facing inwards with short or long arm hold; note how centrifugal force/swirl of water enlarges circle. Try a train and encourage hoots and whistles with an occasional stop at the station (poolside).

46. The Snake – where's that tail! and someone is not so happy – but no doubt relieved to know that his helper is securing him by holding through onto the helper in front.

6   RING A RING O' ROSES

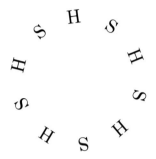

Formation Swimmers and helpers alternate in a circle, all facing the centre.

Description The circle moves to the right chanting the rhyme as follows:

>Ring a ring o' (bubbles)
>A pocket full of (bubbles)
>Atishoo, atishoo, we all (sit on pool bottom)

This is repeated with the circle moving in the opposite direction.

Teaching points Head control and breathing control.

Checking points Water adjustment and breathing control.

Variations 'Baa baa black sheep' or any other song that comes to mind is used, blowing bubbles at the end of each line.

Count up to 20 while moving round the circle. Start with a short arm hold and progress if possible to a long arm hold. At the count of 5, 10, 15, and 20 everyone blows bubbles and submerges their head. Then move round the other way and count down from 20.

47. Ring a Ring o' Roses – push down in the water with your shoulders.
48. Ring a Ring o' Roses – the group in the circle have all 'fallen down'.

7   CATCHING TOES

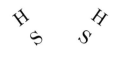

Formation Swimmers in front of helpers, both facing the middle of circle.

Description Swimmers lie back in the water, toes all touching in centre. On 'Go' swimmers stand up quickly and try to catch someone else's toes.

Teaching points Breathing control, and head control resulting in a forward recovery.

Checking points Breathing control. Use of head, arms and knees to create the forward recovery.

Variations Swimmers alternate with helpers while in a circle. At 'Go' the helpers withdraw all support as the swimmers endeavour to catch each other's toes. 'Eggs for breakfast' (see photographs 49, 50 and 51), where swimmers 'go to sleep' as they lie back. On waking up they catch 'poached eggs' instead of toes.

49. Eggs for Breakfast – back float 'go to bed' and safe breathing position; helpers give minimum support at point of balance.
50. Eggs for Breakfast – the half way stage. Note the head forward starts the vertical rotation as hands reach for the 'eggs'.
51. Eggs for Breakfast – grab those eggs. Swimmers have just (unconsciously perhaps) performed a vertical rotation.

8   DING DONG BELL

Formation Swimmers and helpers in a circle, facing inwards.

Description Swimmers are held on short arm hold and encouraged to balance their bodies in the vertical position. Feet off the floor; chin on knees. 'Ding' – the head moves backwards (see photograph 52). 'Dong' – the head moves forwards, the swimmer blows bubbles (see photograph 53). This must be a very slow movement.

Teaching points Forward rolls, backward rolls. Breathing control. Vertical rotation.

Checking points Head control. The helper may assist the balance of the swimmer by lowering the short arm hold downwards deeper in the water. The reverse will cause the head to move backwards.

Variations Progress to the use of the long arm hold where the swimmer has more control over the movements of his own body.

52. Ding Dong Bell – heads back and knees up.
53. Ding Dong Bell – heads forward, and the body has performed a 180°
    (almost) vertical rotation. A prime example of head control.

9   FOOTBALL MATCH

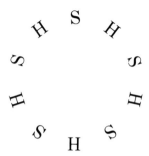

Formation A circle is formed with the swimmer to one side of the helper, linking arms.

Description This game is based on a visit to a football match. Everybody pushes to the middle and jostling and barging occurs as they go through the turnstiles. Once inside the 'gate' the circle enlarges. This is repeated for occasions such as goals, half time and full time.

Teaching points Head and breathing control.

Checking points Water adjustment, breathing control. Also check that the swimmers' heads are forward when moving backwards.

Variations 'Rugby match'. As above, except that scrums and mauls are simulated by trying to push the other side of the circle backwards.

10 MUSICAL CHAIRS

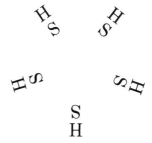

Formation Circle in pairs, all facing inwards. Swimmer sitting on helper's knee; helper balanced in chair position. Swimmer's hands and arms floating towards the centre of the circle.

Description The object is for the swimmer to be rotated in the vertical position from helper to helper round the circle. Each helper offers his right arm, rotating the swimmer onto his knee, holding the whole right arm of the swimmer approaching his knee. The swimmer assists the helper by offering his right arm, turning his head. The swimmers are moved round the circle on the word 'Change' (given by the group leader).

Having progressed back to the original helper, the process is reversed. The helper's left arm takes the left arm of the swimmer on his left.

Teaching points Adjustment to water. Lateral rotation in vertical position. Balance.

11 SHOOTING THE RAPIDS

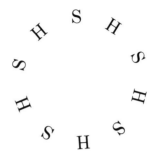

Formation Circle; helpers standing, palms upwards, on extended arms with swimmers floating on backs looking at ceiling with palms downwards and feet pointed towards centre of circle.

Description Best swimmer goes first as an example to others. Two helpers on either side walk forwards as swimmer in between becomes a canoe (see photograph 54). Swimmer pushes head well back to keep toes on surface and 'shoots' across extended arms on other side of circle, hollowing his back so as not to scrape the canoe's bottom on the rocks. After his bottom is over the arms (rapids) he completes a forward recovery (see photograph 55) and stands up; then with head back he allows the two helpers to draw him back across the rapids back to his position in the circle and stands up. Move round the circle with two 'shoots' for each swimmer.

Teaching points Lie still and maintain balance in water; head well back in water facilitates leg flotation; forward recovery (vertical rotation) after crossing rapids and again when back in the circle.

Checking points As arms are held, swimmer must accentuate head movement to complete forward recovery and 'blow bubbles'; head back on return and watch those legs float up.

54. Shooting the Rapids – stage one, with head back the swimmer becomes a canoe. Note the sock for protection.
55. Shooting the Rapids – the canoe has 'shot the rapids' and now standing up is simply a forward recovery.

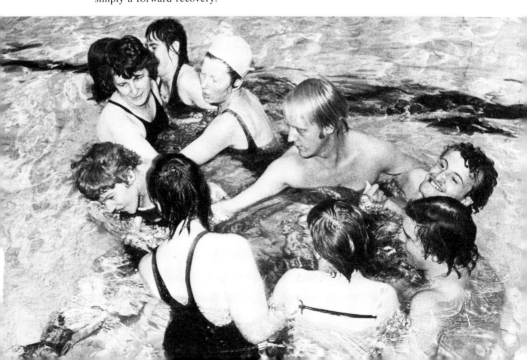

12 ROLLING ROUND THE CIRCLE

Formation Swimmers in front of helpers, who form a circle.
Description Swimmers lie back in bed and the helper supports the swimmer on his left hand. On 'Go' the swimmers do a full lateral rotation to their left. The helper then moves towards the swimmer coming to him. The helpers should concentrate on the swimmer to be received (see photograph 56). After a full circuit, change direction. If required, the rotation is aided by the helper taking the swimmer's arm above the elbow after the swimmer has started the roll. With an extra helper, the game is eased as only one swimmer need rotate at once, towards the spare helper.
Teaching points Lateral rotations.
Checking points Breathing control.
Variations As an introduction to the lateral rotation, a rubber ring may be passed clockwise from one swimmer's right hand to another's right hand, thus inducing a ¼ roll and recovery (see photograph 57). Various songs can be used to determine the rate of rotation. 'There were ten in the bed and the last one said – roll over . . . There were nine . . .'

56. Rolling round the Circle – note the useful spare helper and attention to arrivals not departures.
57. Rolling round the Circle – a variation of the game using rubber rings.

13 SPACESHIPS

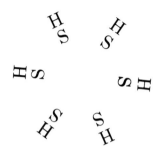

Formation Circle; helpers outside facing swimmers on inside. Helpers envelop swimmers with arms supporting round swimmer's back or waist as necessary. Swimmers are thus safely 'docked' in spaceship/capsule.

Description At 'Go' the swimmer twists the helper's ear to release the spaceship for his 'Moon Walk'. The helper's arms then open and release the swimmer to walk or clamber a full circuit round the stationary helper and back into dock; another twist of the ear and the arms close and the spaceship has returned safely to dock.

Teaching points Excellent for water adjustment, confidence and disengagement; starting by gripping the helper's wrist and wriggling round, the swimmer progresses to total independence by not touching the helper at all.

Checking points Breathing control. Balance.

Variations As swimmers advance they can 'space walk', clockwise and anti-clockwise (having to think which.is which takes the swimmer's mind off fear), round the whole circle of helpers. First stage with helper's extended arms linked, later unlinked.

58.   Spaceships – unlocking the 'space capsule'.

14 FISHES IN THE NET

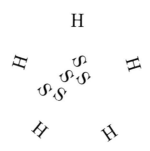

Formation The helpers form a circle, holding hands. The swimmers are in the circle with extra support from other helpers or more able swimmers.

Description On the call 'Fishes out' the swimmers leave the circle by ducking under the arms of the helpers. Once outside they hold onto the circle. Depending on ability, swimmers re-enter the circle one at a time or all together over the arms of the circle (see photograph 59). They achieve this by using a combined rotation to dive over the arms (this puts them onto their backs), and then a vertical rotation so as to become upright and standing again.

Teaching points Water happiness, head control, breathing control, combined and vertical rotations.

Checking points All the teaching points, especially breathing control after the vertical rotation.

Variations This game can be made harder if the circle moves round at varying pace.

59. Fishes in the Net – after escaping from the net, the swimmers now perform a combined rotation in returning over the net and finally a forward recovery to stand up.

60.   Gala time – trophies, medals and competitors await the prizegiving whilst an official checks her bathside record sheet and the announcer gives the results of the last race.

Chapter Twelve
Gala Organisation

Whether at club, area or national level, the aim of organising a gala is to produce a programme which is fair to the swimmers, interesting to both swimmers and spectators, and practical as far as the officials are concerned. It is essential that it is run in a smooth and efficient pattern which will encourage those taking part to do themselves justice, be it in the water or on the bathside.

The method of timed handicap racing is designed to ensure that each swimmer has an equal chance of winning according to his ability. The slowest swimmer starts at 'Go', and other competitors at time intervals obtained by deducting their time for the distance from that of the slowest swimmer. In theory the race will be a dead heat. It is accepted that there could be an improvement of performance, within reasonable limits, under competition conditions, and therefore an improvement allowance is permitted – usually up to three seconds per length. However, if a swimmer improves by more than the improvement allowance he is disqualified. The principle is to stop swimmers using unfair advantage or gamesmanship, or club handicappers 'helping' their own club swimmers. Certificates of achievement are given to swimmers who improve by more than the allowance, and are a record of their improved time.

The first meeting of the gala committee should take place about four months before the gala; its first task should be to elect a gala organiser. A venue, date and time for the gala should then be fixed, which must be confirmed in writing as soon as possible with the baths authorities. A letter is then sent with these details and entry forms

ENTRY FORM

For: ....

To be held at: ....

On .... day   Date: ....   Time: ....   For: .... start

The swimmers listed below are from .... A.S.T.R.A./club

Event	Swimmer & Club	*Special care info	Time entered min	sec	Reserve Swimmer & Club	*Special care info	Time entered min	sec
Girls' 1 length								
Boys' 1 length								
Ladies' 1 length								
Men's 1 length								
Girls' Championship								
Boys' Championship								
Ladies' Championship								
Men's Championship								
Junior Team Race 4 x 1 length of the Club	1 2 3 4				Individual reserves	Club		
	Total							
Senior Team Race 4 x 1 length of the Club	1 2 3 4				Individual reserves	Club		
	Total							

Name of team manager .... who shall bring 1 copy to the Gala.

This form has been completed by ....

address .... Tel no ....

PLEASE RETURN ONE COPY OF THIS FORM WHEN COMPLETED TO: ....

address .... Tel no ....

who is the championship handicapper, by (date) ....

Please inform the handicapper by telephone of any late changes, and confirm in writing and hand to him at the baths on arrival.

After entry forms have been submitted, alterations for individual events must be made no later than ..... a.m./p.m. on .... whilst for team races alterations can be made up to ..... a.m./p.m. on .... (using Form K).

The length of the pool is .... thus the championship race will be...... lengths.

All swimmers must be first claim within the Region.

A swimmer may not enter more than one individual event and a team race in these Championships

A Junior is one under 17 years of age on 1 January 19...

No Junior may swim in a Senior event or vice versa.

* Please use the following abbreviations for any swimmer who requires SPECIAL CARE:-

  B - blind   D - deaf   E - epileptic   PS - requires a prompt start

  WH - uses a wheelchair   IA - instructor accompanied in water

Please use an asterisk with a note below for any other instructions not mentioned above.

(see example facing) to the clubs selected. (The number of clubs invited may well depend on the number of lanes available in the pool, unless the committee is prepared to run heats.) Ensure you include the time the doors will open for officials, for swimmers and when the racing will start, together with an estimated finishing time. The length of the pool in both yards and metres should be shown clearly so that the entered times will be accurate.

Any relevant information about access to the baths, car parking and transport facilities, and a map, will be useful, as some may be visiting the baths for the first time. This information should be made available to the team managers and officials. It is advisable to have a tear-off slip indicating acceptance and which events will be entered, or a refusal. This should be returned by a fixed date so that others can be invited in good time to replace any refusals.

Fix a date by which all trophies must be returned before the gala. Enclose two copies of the entry form with each invitation: when both are completed one copy should be sent to the handicapper by a specified date, the other copy should be given to the team manager who should bring it to the gala for his own use.

The entry form should have space to record the list of events in programme order, the name and club of the competitor, and their entered time – usually the fastest time over the distance. A space should be provided to show any special care details of the individual swimmers. The closing date and time for alterations, the address and telephone number of the handicapper to whom the form should be sent, and the name and telephone number of the team manager are also vital.

The committee should also draw up a list of officials (see overleaf) who should be contacted by the gala organisers. Those who have accepted should be sent a sheet of instructions for their particular job three weeks before the gala. Supplies of these instructions to officials, together with other examples of gala forms, can be obtained from the A.S.T. The officials' instructions have a common heading detailing venue, date and time of gala, and naming the other officials; all this information is completed by the gala organiser. He must also send to each team manager, a week before the gala, the instructions for the gala, duly completed, along with a form for team and spectator comments, which could be completed and returned after the gala.

A programme will be necessary, giving the list of events with spaces

OFFICIALS' CHECK-IN LIST

Gala liaison officer ....

Announcer ....

* Starter ....

* Check starter ....

* Chief judge ....

+ Place judge .... Turn judge ....

* Referee ....

* Chief timekeeper .... Runner ....

       Timekeeper 1. .... 2. ....

                3. .... 4. ....

                5. .... 6. ....

Handicapper .... Runner ....

Assistant Handicapper .... Typing ....

Recorder ....

Assistant recorder ....

Chief whip .... Runner ....

Assistant Whip ....

Trophy Steward 1. .... 2. ....

Host to presenters ....

Officials' check-in (Gala Liaison Officer)

                    ....

Competitors' check-in (Recorder)

                    ....

Programme sellers 1. .... 2. ....

Bathside supervisor .... Bathside steward 1. ....

Water safety team leader .... 2. ....

Dressing room ....

Hospitality & Refreshments ....

Spectators' usher ....

Reception for guests ....

Car park attendant ....

Hon Medical adviser ....

Scoreboard ....

Raffle tickets ....

* large clip board needed

+ small clip board needed

All officials should have badges carrying their name and title.

for the first, second and third placings. Some rules of the competition and the points system used should be given. A short history of the club or Region can be added, and details of future events and invitations for offers of help to the club may be included. The committee should decide whether to charge for the programme. Some clubs raise money by holding a raffle at the gala and therefore do not charge for admission or for programmes. If you decide to hold a raffle, you must first check with the baths manager that it is permitted, then make arrangements for the prizes, raffle books and a team of ticket sellers, and arrange for the timing of the draw.

The gala committee should also decide which guests should be invited, whether a reception is to be given and what refreshments should be served. Biscuits and hot drinks for the competitors may suffice for a small local gala, but obviously the larger the gala, the greater the number of guests, and the more ambitious the refreshments. It is a good idea to provide each guest with a host who knows something of the organisation and can explain any details about the gala. It is also an ideal opportunity to entertain and discuss the activities of your club with those who can help you. Problems of transport and 'pool time' could here be raised in the atmosphere of a well-run and happy occasion.

On arrival at the baths for the gala, each swimmer should report to his team manager, who should check him on the entry form. It is the

COMPETITORS' CHECK-IN LIST FOR USE BY THE RECORDER

Event No	Club / ASTRA							
1								
2								
3								
4								
5								
6								
7								
8								
9								
10								

● Competitors in individual events who also appear in relays need only appear ONCE on this sheet, under their individual event

Junior Relay								
Senior Relay								
Team Manager								
Time Keeper								

team manager's duty to keep the recorder informed about the arrival of swimmers. The recorder will be at the table on the bathside so that he can work with the handicapper in preparation for the start. The recorder uses a competitors' check-in list, which is a list of clubs, team managers and swimmers made up from the entry forms. It is essential that the recorder is informed by each team manager the moment his own team is complete and that any absentees or changes made in the relays have been recorded. A closing time for changes of time and swimmers in individual events – normally the day before the gala – should be shown on the entry forms. It is usual to accept changes for time and/or swimmers in the relays up to fifteen minutes before the gala: this avoids disappointing the remainder of the team if one swimmer drops out.

All officials on arrival at the gala should check in with the gala organiser before going to the bathside. They should receive lapel badges with their names and duties; some will need clipboards to hold the bathside record sheets. Ushers stand at the main doors to direct spectators, swimmers and guests, and to distribute programmes to all visitors.

Bathside record sheets (see opposite), which control the whole of the Association of Swimming Therapy's method of timed handicap racing, can be obtained from the Association. The sheets are in five colours, each event has six sheets, either typed or handwritten, with carbon paper. The first three sheets of pink are for the starter, check starter and chief judge. The referee has a blue sheet, the whips a green sheet and the chief timekeeper a yellow sheet. The white sheets are only used once racing has started, to show an alteration; they take precedence over the coloured sheets.

The handicapper completes the master bathside record sheets for each event as soon as he receives all the entries from the clubs. He enters all the names of the swimmers for an event, in club order, on the left-hand side. If there are more swimmers than lanes available he will have to run heats, made up of approximately equal numbers of swimmers. He then enters the swimmers on the right-hand side of the form, starting at the top with the slowest entered time and ending with the fastest. He calculates each swimmer's 'go at' time (the slowest starts at 'go'), and deducts the entered time of the remainder from the slowest entered time. The disqualification time, in its simplest form, is calculated by deducting up to three seconds per

BATHSIDE RECORD SHEET

_____ _____ Club   _____ 19____

Event _____   Heat _____ / Final

Swimmer	Team	Time		Go at		Result				
		m	s	m	s	Aggregate m s	Place	Actual m	s	

Disqualify all aggregate times less than ____ m ____ s

MASTER BATHSIDE RECORD SHEET

_____ Club   _____ 19____

Event(s)_____   Heats / Final

Swimmer	Team	Time entered m s	Time swum m s	Swimmer	Team	Time m s	Go at m s
			Disqualify all aggregate times less than ____ m ____ s		HEAT 1	
			Disqualify all aggregate times less than ____ m ____ s		HEAT 2	

Finish: shallow / deep

length from the slowest swimmer's entered time. The usual deduction for a four-length relay is nine seconds.

When the latest time for alterations has passed (normally the day before the gala), the bathside record sheets can be prepared from the master bathside record sheets, completing columns 1 to 4. The handicapper's first duty at the gala is to amend the bathside record sheet, noting any known non-starter and making any amendments to relays. Only then can the whips be given their green bathside record sheets to enable them to call the swimmers for the first race. Next the runners should take the remaining sheets to the other officials and the gala can start.

The sequence of events leading up to, during, and after a race can be followed on the flow chart (see p. 134). The whips use their green bathside record sheets to collect the swimmers for the race from their poolside station (any entered swimmer who is absent should be clearly marked as a non-starter). The green bathside record sheet then goes to the announcer. The swimmers are taken to the check starter who shows them to their race lane in the order of his pink bathside record sheet, even if this results in gaps due to the absence of swimmers. The starter informs each swimmer of the 'go at' time and takes up his position next to the fastest lane. When he is satisfied that all is in order, the gala organiser will instruct the announcer to start the gala with the information for the first race set out on his green bathside record sheet. As the announcement is being made, the check starter brings the swimmers to their starting positions, either at the bathside or in the water. The starter then takes over, calling the officials to order as follows: 'Timekeeper, judges, referee'. Each raises his hand to signify readiness. Then 'Swimmers' and, if they are ready, 'Take your marks', pause, 'Go'. At 'Go' all official watches should be started. The starter then counts aloud the time elapsing, in seconds from his watch, until all the swimmers have started. Whilst this is taking place the check starter moves along the line of swimmers and alerts each one when his 'go at' time is reached, according to his bathside record sheet (this will also show certain disabilities, e.g. deaf, which may well require a 'prompt start' i.e. a tap on the shoulder and an exhortation to *go!*

61. Gala time – more disabled competitors enoy a race with helpers behind so as not to create turbulence (this would assist the swimmer to a faster time).

The referee, during this count-down, notes on his blue bathside record sheet that each swimmer has started on time, while at the end of the race he notes any swimmer who touches before or near the disqualification time, and the aggregate time of the first and last swimmers, as a double check. The chief timekeeper confirms that all

BATHSIDE RECORD SHEET: FLOW CHART

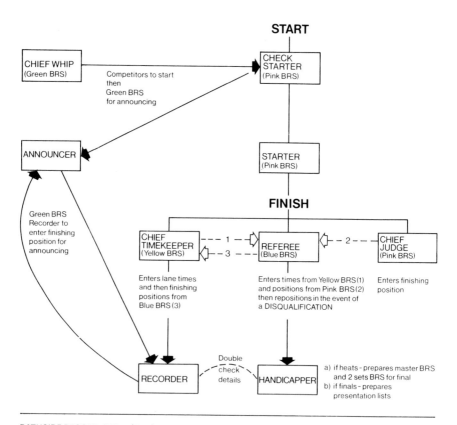

BATHSIDE RECORD SHEET (BRS) Colours

1st set 1. Pink – starter
2. Pink – check starter
3. Pink – chief judge

2nd set 1. Blue – referee
2. Green – chief whip
3. Yellow – chief timekeeper

RUNNERS

referee and chief timekeeper
chief whip
handicapper

62. Gala time – the starter here moves from lane to lane giving the staggered
start which theoretically results in the race ending in a dead heat.

the watches of his timekeepers actually started at 'Go'. If the chief timekeeper's watch is 'free' he should stop it when the last swimmer finishes; if it is a two-button watch, he should stop it on the first and last swimmers as they finish. It is prudent for all timekeepers to test their stop watches for uniformity before races start; and clearly during races if there is a suspicion of malfunction.

After each race the chief timekeeper records in the fifth column on the yellow bathside record sheet the aggregate time from each lane timekeeper, double-checking by reading their watches himself. At the same time the chief judge confers with the place and turn judges, then enters the final agreed finishing order in the sixth column of the pink bathside record sheet. The referee copies the times from the chief timekeeper into the fifth column of his blue bathside record sheet, and the place, from the judge, into the sixth column. The judge must mark a 'D' in the sixth column against any swimmer who is disqualified either on time or for any other reason, adjusting the finishing order accordingly. These positions are then checked by the chief timekeeper who records them in the sixth column of his yellow bathside record sheet.

Yellow and blue bathside record sheets are now identical, so the runner takes the yellow one to the recorder and the blue to the handicapper, who are sitting at the same table as the announcer. The recorder and handicapper confer, cross-checking the times and placings on both bathside record sheets.

The recorder takes the yellow sheet and fills in the places and any disqualifications on the green bathside record sheet, which the runner gave the announcer before the start of the race. He then uses it to announce the result at a suitable time; he may, at about the same time, receive the green sheet for the next race and should announce that as well. However, the announcer must never announce the next race before the final result is out, that being when the yellow sheet is with the recorder. The announcing of a race is the signal for the whole operation to start again, and by using this method swimmers are prevented from entering the water and thus getting cold before they need.

Meanwhile, the handicapper and recorder agree the swimmer's 'actual time' ('aggregate time' less the 'go at' time), and enter this in the seventh column of their bathside record sheets. The recorder then completes his master results sheet (opposite) which should be

A.S.T.

Master Results Sheet

Points System:
First place in a final	4 points
Second place in a final	3 points
Third place in a final	2 points
Fourth place in a final	1 point

Key

Event / Name	Club	Time			Res.	Area/Club points				Row Total
		Entered	Swum							
		m s	m s	b/f						
	Disq. Allow. [ ] Secs.			b/f						
	Disq. Allow. [ ] Secs.			b/f						
	Disq. Allow. [ ] Secs.			b/f						
	Disq. Allow. [ ] Secs.			Points Totals						

photocopied and sent to all competing clubs for their records. If certificates of achievement (see below) are to be given to those swimmers disqualified on time, these should be prepared by the recorder and given to the team managers concerned after the gala.

ASSOCIATION OF SWIMMING THERAPY

ASTRA ONE

CHAMPIONSHIPS

Awarded to _____ on _____

for swimming a distance of _____ in __ mins __ secs

being an improvement on their entered time of __ mins __ secs

_____

When there are heats the handicapper makes out a master bathside record sheet from the heats to make up the final, from which the bathside record sheets are prepared. The sheets are then distributed to the relevant officials by the runners. During the gala the handicapper completes four copies of a trophy and medal winners list for use by the host to presenters, trophy stewards, announcer and chief whip at the presentations.

The presentations, usually at the end of the gala, are organised by the trophy steward and the host to presenters, while the whip arranges the swimmers in order.

A meeting after the gala to discuss shortcomings and improvements should lead to higher standards next time.

The whole matter is not as complex as it might appear; but team work and efficient organisation are essential ingredients for a happy and successful gala. If you are organising your first club gala, make it small and short and, as in all else, learn from experience.

Chapter Thirteen
Training Courses

The Association of Swimming Therapy is structured as shown below; it is divided for administrative purposes into regions known as A.S.T.R.A.s. The Education Committee is responsible for training courses.

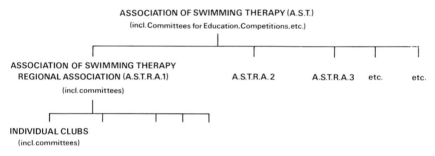

ASSOCIATION OF SWIMMING THERAPY (A.S.T.)
(incl. Committees for Education, Competitions, etc.)

ASSOCIATION OF SWIMMING THERAPY REGIONAL ASSOCIATION (A.S.T.R.A.1) (incl. committees) A.S.T.R.A.2 A.S.T.R.A.3 etc. etc.

INDIVIDUAL CLUBS
(incl. committees)

GENERAL

Training courses are vital to the spread of knowledge and experience that are set out in this book. However, the knowledge acquired on a course is of little value if it is not regularly practised at your weekly club sessions. We have tried to stress the importance of practical experience throughout. Thus much groundwork can and should be carried out in the pool, when the disabled have left, by the chief helper each week.

In order that all who wish can attend courses these should be held on a regular basis and be well publicised. Ultimately the responsibility for education lies with the Education Committee of the A.S.T. Their task is to:

1. Fix dates and arrange advanced training courses.
2. Test and qualify lecturers and demonstrators in the method.

3. Produce as necessary any leaflets, visual aids, equipment, slides, films, video tapes and publications to further the method.
4. Ensure that Regional Education Committees carry their fair share of work and fix their own regular basic courses and tests to qualify club helpers.

COURSE TYPES

1. Basic course
These are the responsibility of the Regional Educational Committee and may be arranged as:
a. One weekend (2 days) with at least 3 hours of pool work.
b. Two weekends (4 days) with at least 6 hours of pool work.
c. 6 or 8 weeks – allowing one night per week of which 1 hour should be in the pool.

We have set out below a suggested two-day course programme, but this is by no means a rigid formula.

First day
9.00 Enrolment and introduction
9.30 Lecture: Philosophy and background
10.00 Lecture: Stage 1: Adjustment to water
10.30 Coffee break and to pool
10.45 Pool: Safety and handling/Entries and exits
      a. Demonstration
      b. Teaching
      c. Practice
12.30 Lunch break
1.15 Lecture: Effect of handicaps in the water
2.00 Lecture: Principles of water physics, shape and density
2.30 Lecture 3: Stage 2: Three rotations
3.00 Pool: Practical of above.
      a. Demonstration
      b. Teaching
      c. Practice
4.30 Tea break and change
5.00 Discussion groups and questions
5.30 Close of day

Second day

9.30	Résumé and programme for the day
9.45	Lecture: Importance of groups
10.15	Lecture: Teaching by games
10.45	Coffee break and to pool
11.00	Pool: a. Stage 3: Upthrust/buoyancy/balance
	b. Games based on Stages 1 – 3
12.30	Lunch break
1.15	Lecture: Progress of a swimmer and competition
1.30	Proficiency tests allied to the 4 stages
2.00	Group exercise: Programme preparation in groups for a swimming session (given age/ability/badge level/etc.)
2.30	Pool: Practical application of above
	Stage 4: Propulsion and effects of turbulence
4.00	Tea break and change
4.30	Film: *Water Free*
5.00	Summary: Certificates of attendance
	Close of course

2.   Advanced courses

These are properly the responsibility of the National Education Committee and will cover the following topics:

a. Games, their use and purpose.
b. Programmes for progress.
c. Importance and study of groups
d. Water safety and resuscitation.
e. Competition methods.
f. Deep end programme.
g. Training and demonstrators, lecturers and helpers.
h. Invigilation for club helper certificate.

3.   Gala procedure course

Galas are most popular events and their enjoyment for swimmers and spectators can be marred by inefficient organisation. These courses are of great value in learning to run your galas efficiently.

ADVICE ON RUNNING A COURSE

The first obvious prerequisite is to establish an adequate demand and then make firm arrangements for a pool. Try to find a pool that is large enough and with adequate depth, together, ideally with a nearby lecture room plus extra class room. The water temperature should not be less than 80°F. Those wishing to attend should be notified well in advance and the early payment of a small sum to cover expenses such as coffee and biscuits etc. usually ensures that few drop out at the last minute.

As in the well-organised club you will need helpers and arrangements for refreshments; and somewhere to sit and eat should be made available. Clearly there may be need for sleeping accommodation on two- or four-day courses. Do give careful thought to numbers attending – neither too few as to disappoint the voluntary helpers and lecturers, nor too many as to spoil the effectiveness of the groups that should be carefully planned beforehand.

Course members should bring: notebook and pen, two swimming suits and towels, track suit or bathwrap, and bathside shoes.

USEFUL ADDRESSES

Association of Swimming Therapy, 1 Buchan Grove, Crewe, Cheshire.

National Association of Swimming Clubs for the Handicapped, 63 Dunvegan Road, Eltham, London SE9.

The Sports Council, 70 Brompton Road, London SW3 1EX.

Chapter Fourteen
Helper Education

When this book was proposed there was a widespread fear that it would produce 'armchair' experts without adequate practical experience. So once again we stress that experience in your regular club session is of paramount importance. A great deal can be learnt from intelligent observation of experienced helpers at work and even more by joining them in the pool, with group games etc. The best helpers will try to pass on their wisdom and experience, seeking to encourage new helpers to join in and take an increasingly active part in the responsibility of pool work.

Helper education should be a natural part of your weekly session; it will develop a spirit of camaraderie, enabling experience to be exchanged. Often new helpers can be encouraged to discuss matters freely at informal social gatherings of swimmers and helpers after the club session. Moreover, as the years of experience are accumulated, the theoretical aspects of physics will become both better understood and more meaningful.

A.S.T. CLUB INSTRUCTOR'S CERTIFICATE

Conditions of Examination
Prerequisite conditions
Candidates for examination must have:
a. Completed a period of 100 hours active *club* instruction.
b. A certificate of attendance at a Basic Course.
c. A recommendation from their club committee.
d. A basic knowledge of bathside and water safety.

Practical examination
Candidates will be required to show ability in the following:
a. Assist correct entries and exits to and from the water.
b. Demonstrate correct holds backing and facing swimmer.

c. Demonstrate ability in circle work, using short- and long-arm holds.

d. Demonstrate correct holds from the side of the swimmer as for lateral rotations.

e. Demonstrate intelligent use of disengagement.

f. Demonstrate personal ability in A.S.T. green badge test.

g. Follow a group leader and communicate properly with a disabled swimmer in the water.

Viva Voce examinations

Candidates will be expected to have a knowledge of and be able to give clear explanations of:

a. Breathing control and its development.

b. The Four Stages: adjustment – rotations – buoyancy – propulsion; and their development.

c. Bathside and club safety drill.

d. Use of groups, games and teaching methods.

e. Badge tests and their practical application.

On completion of the test the successful candidate will be awarded a certificate. This should be endorsed each year to ensure that the helper keeps in touch and up to date.

A.S.T. LECTURERS

It is clear that these will be drawn from the ranks of those with very extensive experience, who will probably have served for many years on their club, regional or national committees. They will have been chief or senior helpers in their clubs for long periods, well accustomed to the tasks of a group leader in the water; they will probably have officiated at regional and national galas.

They should have acquired an overall knowledge of the subject and an ability to answer questions on A.S.T. topics. They should be able to preplan a programme carefully and thoroughly, and discipline themselves to stick to the subject and not over-run the allotted time. They should also be able to impart knowledge clearly, in an interesting manner – with the use of examples and visual aids to avoid boredom. Finally, they must aim to encourage, never discourage, and stimulate audience participation. Most of the benefits of the lecture will be lost if those attending do not put into practice, actively and regularly, what they have learnt – this should be stressed.

DEMONSTRATORS

Good, knowledgeable and enthusiastic demonstrators are an invaluable aid to lecturers both in and out of the water. Their sure demonstrations will both aid the understanding of the course members and also provide the demonstrators with excellent experience when they, perhaps, graduate to becoming lecturers themselves.